MEMOIRS OF A JAZZ-AGE
BABE

MEMOIRS OF A JAZZ-AGE BABE

Arthur Butler

Book Guild Publishing
Sussex, England

First published in Great Britain in 2013 by
The Book Guild Ltd
Pavilion View
19 New Road
Brighton, BN1 1UF

Typesetting in Garamond by
Keyboard Services, Luton, Bedfordshire

Printed in Great Britain by
CPI Group (UK) Ltd, Croydon, CR0 4YY

A catalogue record for this book is available from
The British Library

ISBN 978 1 84624 902 0

To Ella and Fred –
no son could ever have had more loving
and supportive parents

Contents

1 Jazz-Age Babe   1

2 Soldier Mad   25

3 No Passage to India   45

4 Great Brittain   71

5 Man of the World   89

6 The Forlorn Hope   123

Epilogue: Mail from the Front Line   143

Bibliography   147

Index   149

1

Jazz-Age Babe

'Look Arthur! The princesses are playing in the garden.' My mother's voice rose in excitement and I quickly moved over to her side on the upper deck of the London bus. We were passing 145 Piccadilly, an imposing house on the approach to Park Lane, home to the Duke and Duchess of York. We were looking down on their children, Princess Elizabeth and her younger sister Margaret. It was 1935. There was a small dog with them – the first in the long line of Welsh corgis owned by the family. It was, the public learnt, called Dookie and it had a reputation for bad temper.

As we had seen on other occasions from the top deck of the bus, their governess, Marion Crawford, was also in the high-walled enclosure. Known as 'Crawfie', she was to cause public outrage in 1950 when, after being with the family for seventeen years, she wrote a book about them. Compared to what would be written about the royals later, it was relatively harmless. At this still deferential time, however, Crawfie was sharply criticised for a breach of trust and her name became synonymous with gossipy disloyalty.

From the upper windows of the house, Princess Elizabeth could wave to her grandfather King George V across Green Park and the gardens of nearby Buckingham Palace, where he would be watching for her with a pair of field glasses.

Soon, with his death in 1936, the little girls' debonair uncle David – a.k.a. Edward, Prince of Wales – would be proclaimed King. He would, of course, abdicate before his coronation in order to marry 'the woman he loved' – the twice-divorced American, Mrs Wallis Simpson. It would be their father, the Duke of York, who was crowned instead, becoming King George VI. The princesses moved to the palace and I was no longer able to watch them play as I rode the bus down Piccadilly on the way to visit my grandmother, Alice, in Grosvenor Square. She was employed there as a cook by wealthy American socialite Caroline Offley Shore, the well-connected widow of an Indian Army general who had known, in the course of his duties, a previous Prince of Wales, later King George V.

Colonel Offley Bohun Stovin Fairless Shore of the 18th (Prince of Wales' own) Tiwana Lancers, a crack Indian Army cavalry regiment, previously named the Bengal Lancers, had married Caroline Sinnickson of Philadelphia in 1908. Known to the family as Lina, she was then thirty-eight, seven years younger than her handsome, but impecunious, soldier husband. In that same year he served as Assistant Military Secretary to Earl Grey, Governor General of Canada, during the celebrations to mark the tercentenary of the founding of Quebec. The festival was attended by George when he was Prince of Wales, together with his wife Princess Mary. Lina cemented her link with the royals when, the following year, the Princess and the Countess of Bradford presented her at court. Following a distinguished military career, General Offley Shore died of pneumonia and heart failure in 1922 at the early age of fifty-nine and, heartbroken by his death, Lina decided to overcome her grief by travelling and maintaining a busy social life.

In the 1930s, she entertained lavishly in a well-placed Grosvenor Square apartment and was horrified to witness the social advancement of her 'jumped-up' compatriot Wallis

Simpson. Wallis was busy setting herself up as a London society hostess in her husband's flat in Bryanston Court, not far from Lina, on the far side of Oxford Street. Her status had received a boost when she too was presented at court in 1931. That evening, Wallis and her husband had attended a party given by Thelma, Viscountess Furness, another American, wife to a bad-tempered, womanising shipping magnate. She was also a friend and neighbour of Lina. At the time, Thelma was the mistress of the Prince of Wales, and created her own redundancy when she introduced him to Wallis. By 1933, Thelma had been usurped and Wallis was intimately ensconced with the heir to the throne.

It was during this time that my grandmother Alice Waller was cooking for Lina at Grosvenor Square. My mother visited her every week from our flat in Walton Street, Chelsea and often took me with her. If Lina was at home, she would ask to see us and it was during one such afternoon's discourse that she filled my mother in on the Prince's affair with Mrs Simpson. Lady Cunard, another Grosvenor Square resident and a close friend of the Prince, had irritated Lina by helping Wallis to become accepted at a certain level of London high society – the self-made level. The great families such as the Londonderrys and Derbys, in whose circle Lina moved, watched in indignant horror as the affair developed.

Stories about the philandering habits of the Prince of Wales had been circulating in London society well before he dropped old flames such as Thelma Furness for pushy Wallis. My future father-in-law, Thomas Luetchford, a chauffeur to members of the aristocracy, had delighted one of our Walton Street gatherings by revealing how Lord Furness, on arriving home in the early hours one winter's morning, found the Prince's bowler hat and overcoat in the hallway. He threw them out to the street in a rage, bellowing; 'Whose bloody things are these?!'

He knew very well whose they were.

This was all information withheld from the public by the press lords.

My grandmother's family had come to England from France in the eighteenth century and their original name was Le Bond. Her father Charles, born in 1837, was a fine but poorly-paid boot and shoemaker. He worked at home in London to supply an upmarket shop on Knightsbridge Green that sold his output to some of the wealthiest men in London. As with many poor people, the family suffered from consumption, TB. Charles's brother had died of the illness. He had seen a son fall ill with it – and now his own health was failing.

My grandmother Alice had been born in 1873 and to help the family income, she was taken away from school at eleven and put to work polishing leather. She hated this and when her father's health improved, she told him she would do it no longer. There was only one alternative for Alice; to go into service.

A man who worked at the Knightsbridge Green shop was asked to help. He duly arranged for Alice to have an interview with a grand family in Eaton Square who needed a girl to train as a parlour maid. On the appointed day Alice, thirteen years old, arrived at the house with her few possessions packed in a wicker basket. She went up the front steps and knocked at the door. It opened suddenly and a voice roared; 'Beggars to the basement – go down the steps!'

Alice clumped down to the basement and a young girl opened the door. She was taken to the servants' hall where she was confronted by the butler – a large, stiff looking man – and the housekeeper, dressed in black. They gave her a long, hard look and then consulted together as Alice waited nervously. The man announced that they had decided to give her a chance to show what she could do. Her first task was to dust a

4

cupboard full of china. But nerves made her clumsy and she dropped two pieces that shattered on the floor. The noise brought the butler running in at the double. Seeing the damage, he ordered her angrily to go. Grabbing her basket, Alice ran back up the basement steps, sobbing loudly. Not knowing what to do next she stood on the pavement with tears running down her face. A carriage drove up and a well-dressed lady got out. Seeing Alice crying, she asked what was wrong. On hearing the story she took her by the hand and led her up the steps to the front door. On entering the house this way, the distraught waif found herself in a beautiful, ornate room. The lady rang a bell and in came the butler whose jaw dropped at seeing little Alice with the mistress of the house. He explained that she would never make a parlour maid but that there was a vacant post in the kitchen. Asked if she would like it, Alice quickly answered 'Yes!'

The lady pulled a cord by the fireplace and in marched a footman, resplendent in a well-cut coat with brass buttons. The lady wrote a note and asked him to give it to the chef and take Alice and her basket with him. Down in the kitchen, they were met by a tall, grey-haired man with a small beard who, after reading the note and asking Alice a few questions, led her into another room where three girls sat eating at a table. Patting her kindly on the head, he informed the group: 'From now on, you four will work together.'

My grandmother's career in service had begun.

The chef, she learnt, was French. He was assisted by two under-chefs. The day started early for the four kitchen maids – they rose at five o'clock. Then it was Alice's job to assist another girl named Agnes to clean the large kitchen range. The other girls, Jane and Nell, cleaned the front and basement steps. All this work, together with scrubbing the kitchen floor, chairs and whitewood table, had to be done by nine. The girls then had to parade in clean aprons with clean faces and well-scrubbed hands for inspection by the head chef. Despite the hard work and long hours, Alice was happy.

As the months and years passed by, she was given more opportunities to cook. At the age of eighteen she was chosen to fill the vacancy when an under-chef left. By now, she had been trained in a whole range of cooking but her favourite work was pastry, cakes and sweets. One day, the chef told her that a Very Important Person was coming to dinner the following week and she was to prepare her finest pudding for the occasion. The guest was Bertie, Prince of Wales (later King Edward VII), and in his honour Alice spent two days preparing a magnificent ice cream concoction filled with her own delicious hand-made chocolates. She had no freezer to help with the task; rather she used a huge wooden bucket in which the ice cream mould was packed around with ice. When the mould was turned out on to a silver dish the head chef declared it to be my grand-mother's masterpiece. The Prince of Wales was delighted, too, and after dinner sent a message to the chef asking for the recipe – and the secret of how the chocolates could be placed in the iced pudding without becoming frozen.

Alice was by then making her name. Leading London hostesses began offering good sums of money to entice her to work for them. But the head chef who had taught her so well advised going freelance – she had, he said, so much talent that she could pick and choose her jobs. She bravely followed his advice and was soon in demand for dinner parties at the fashionable great houses of London and the home counties. Sir Arthur Sullivan, best known for his collaboration with W.S. Gilbert on the popular Savoy light operas and a frequent guest at such houses, declared she was 'the best cook in England'.

Aged twenty-four, she was kept even more busy than usual at the time of the Diamond Jubilee celebrations of Queen

Victoria in June 1897. With so many of the great houses in London seeking to outdo each other with the magnificence of their banquets, she was able to command high fees for her increasingly sought-after services. It was the first time in a thousand years of English monarchs that one had reached sixty years on the throne. Perhaps Alice would be pleased to know that her grandson lived long enough to witness the next Diamond Jubilee in the summer of 2012. What a contrast the two Majesties present – Queen Elizabeth II, at the age of eighty-six, is as dedicated as ever to her duties and has barely slowed down; Victoria, eight years younger at seventy-eight, was so fat and worn out by her grief that she could not climb the great sweep of steps into St Paul's Cathedral. The service of thanksgiving for her reign was instead conducted in the open air, outside Christopher Wren's great church.

Alice, fondly indulging my interest in all things concerning soldiers, recalled for me her meeting with the officer who led the great Jubilee parade. At six feet eight inches in height, Captain Oswald Ames of the 2nd Life Guards was the tallest man in the British Army. He was related to one of the hostesses for whom Alice worked.

Victoria had been created Empress of India in 1876 and the troops on parade that Jubilee day included many magnificent regiments from the subcontinent. Amongst those paying tribute would have been the Bengal Lancers, in which General Offley Shore had served.

Another of her culinary innovations was a pie of boned quails. I was vividly reminded of Alice's gourmet talent when in the 1980s, I watched the Danish film *Babette's Feast*. It told Karen Blixen's story of the French lady chef who arrives in Jutland, a puritan outpost of Norway, as a political refugee – forced out of Paris following the political uprising at the downfall of Napoleon III. To repay her shelter she works as a maid and cook for two sisters, without revealing her past. When she wins the lottery, she offers to cook a splendid meal to honour their late father, through whose kindness she was offered a home. She returns to Paris to source the ingredients required. On her return, fine wines and fabulous delicacies are served up to the luxury-starved locals who are salivating in spite of their Spartan ways. Her speciality, her *pièce de resistance*, is then brought out – *Cailles en Sarcophage*, or Quails in their Coffins. It was one of the dishes that had made my grandmother's name and I wondered if her fame had spread to Scandinavia. Like the mystery of the chocolates buried unfrozen in the ice cream, the diners marvelled at how the tiny birds were boned before being entombed perfectly intact beneath the pastry. But Alice was to take a greater enigma than either of these to her grave.

Out of the kitchen, and with independent means, Alice was enjoying quite a social life. Her good looks won the attention of gentlemen seated round the tables where her renowned creations were served. She had exceptionally beautiful hair and was asked by Selfridges, the Oxford Street department store, to sit in a window brushing her long tresses to promote a new hair product. But in the year 1900, when she was twenty-seven, her carefree life was shattered by two events. Her younger brother Alfred, a private in the East Surrey Regiment, died of illness in the Boer War at the age of twenty-four. They had been very close and when on leave in London, the handsome Alfred had liked nothing better than to walk down the street in his red tunic with his good-looking sister on his arm (see extracts from his letters at the end of this book).

The second event is the one shrouded in mystery, as my grandmother would never reveal the details. What is known is that she gave birth to my mother on 18 July 1901 at St Anne's Convent, Soho. An Italian countess showed exceptional interest in the event, visiting the newborn baby girl and bringing gifts.

She requested, presumably with some authority, that my mother be brought up in the Roman Catholic faith and given the Italian name 'Elizina'. A lawyer to one of the high society families for whom my grandmother cooked, a certain Sir Alfred Burton of Lincoln's Inn, allowed his name to be used on the maintenance order and handled financial arrangements made for Alice. My mother believed that a high-born Italian guest staying at one of the great houses where my grandmother had cooked admitted to fathering the child. To avoid scandal, a cover-up was arranged.

Alice, unmarried and wanting to continue her successful career, found a woman to look after her baby. After some years, she next arranged for her sister Carrie, who lived in Battersea, to give the child a home. Alice rented the front parlour from her and little Elizina – or Ella as she was being called by then – was shut there alone for much of the time. Carrie, who had a cruel streak, kept her short of food and would not allow her to play with her own children. If Ella cried, she beat her with a cane.

Whenever Alice visited the house, she would row with her sister and eventually Carrie told her to go and take 'the brat' with her. Alice took Ella to live with a Mrs Tuffin at 64 Richmond Street, off the Edgware Road. She turned out to be as cruel as Aunt Carrie. She lived over an empty shop with her two children, David and Agnes. She was responsible for keeping the shop clean – a task she promptly transferred to little Ella who had to complete the task before going to school. On getting home she had to change back into her ragged dress. Holding an empty pillowcase, she would wait outside a shop with other poor children, some with bare feet, on the corner of the Edgware Road. At closing time, a man in a large white apron would come out and shout 'Now you kids, one at a time.'

The little waifs filed in to fill their pillowcases with food for tuppence. On a good day they would get pork pies and pieces of chicken. On Saturdays Ella was sent to a baker's shop for stale bread. That was her favourite errand as she also got stale cakes and could have a good feed before she got home. She did all the household's tasks. One night, she collected a basin of faggots and peasepudding for Mrs Tuffin's supper. A boy knocked it out of her hand and she stood looking in horror at the broken crockery and mess at her feet, too frightened to go home. It was bitterly cold. Eventually the old man who owned the shop came out to close up. He took pity on the shivering child, took another basin from his shelf, filled it with faggots and walked round with Ella to explain to Mrs Tuffin what had happened. As soon as he had left she turned on Ella in a fury, beat her severely and sent her to sleep on the floor of the cold, empty shop without any supper.

My grandmother would visit her once a month. Alice took her daughter out to tea and Mrs Tuffin would have Ella dressed up in one of the pretty frocks and shoes that Alice had bought. No sooner was she back at Richmond Street than Mrs Tuffin would have her back in the ragged dress.

One morning when Ella had finished cleaning the shop, Mrs Tuffin announced she could not go to school that day as she had more chores to do. She then appeared with her apron full of oranges and told Ella to take off her shoes and stockings. She put the oranges in a basket and told her to go to Bell Street nearby and sell the fruit to passers-by – two for a penny. Standing barefoot on the draughty corner, she sold a few but Mrs Tuffin had told her not to return until she had got rid of them all. Cold and miserable, she began to cry. A lady and gentleman took pity on the wretched little girl and declared they would buy all she had left. They filled a bag with oranges and the man put a coin in her hand. When she showed it to

Mrs Tuffin, the ghastly woman was delighted. It was a half sovereign. To Ella's horror, she cackled; 'You'll go again tomorrow. You're going to be lucky for me!'

The year was now 1910. Ella was eight. People were discussing the health of King Edward VII – the man who had grown fat on her mother's ice cream pudding. Then came the announcement – the King was dead. As George V was proclaimed the new monarch, men started to build stands in Oxford Street for his father's funeral procession. They were draped in black and purple cloth. Ella, like all school children, had a holiday from school on the day of the funeral, but Mrs Tuffin soon found more work for her to do. Together with a neighbour's three children, she was instructed to go to Oxford Street – not far from Paddington – and as soon as the cortège had passed, to strip the cloth from the stands.

'Get the purple stuff – not the black,' ordered Mrs Tuffin and off ran the children to enjoy themselves. As the crowds dispersed, the scrawny pipsqueaks stripped the fabric as fast as their hands could grab at it. London bobbies shouted at them and gave chase, truncheons waving, but they soon tired of that and let the children escape with their spoils. In time, most of the windows in run-down Richmond Street were seen to sport pristine new purple curtains.

Some months after the King's funeral came August holiday time. News arrived that Ella's grandmother had died. Since her husband's death, the old lady had been living with another daughter, Nell, in Dover. Alice told Mrs Tuffin she would be taking Ella, now aged nine, to the funeral.

In Dover, Alice explained to her sister Nell that although she would be returning to London that evening, she would like Ella to spend time there during the holidays. Declaring that Ella looked as though she could do with a good feed, Nell agreed that she could stay. Ella met her five cousins for the first time – Charlie, who was older than her, and Alice, George, May and Alfred, all younger. As the children played in an upstairs room after lunch, May accidentally hit Ella on the back. She cried out in pain. Nell ran upstairs and when she saw Ella's back, called for Alice to come and see. It was scarred and covered with weals from the continual beatings Mrs Tuffin gave her. Nell noticed too how filthy Ella's head was and turning on her sister, shouted angrily that the poor mite was not going back to that 'wicked woman'.

When Nell's husband, George Rawlings, returned home from work and the facts were explained he, too, agreed that Ella should stay at Dover. At last, a happy new chapter had opened for her. Until then, she had been lonely and unloved. Her mother had shown her no affection and nor did she ever, perhaps because she was resentful of the stigma Ella brought her, perhaps because her own young life had been hard. Whatever the reason, Ella bore no grudge and would care for Alice as she got older. During her final days – having set her bed on fire once too often with the cigarettes that kept her alive well into her nineties – Alice drifted in and out of consciousness. Ella wet her mother's lips with brandy. The formidable old lady, long since known to all as 'Blossom' after a famously cantankerous radio character of the day, opened her eyes. 'Thank you darling,' she murmured. Ella, herself in her sixties by then, looked over her shoulder to see if someone else had entered the room. It was the only loving word Alice had ever uttered to her daughter.

But for now, she was to become part of a warm and loving (if impoverished) home. The man of the house was George, a smart, good-looking man who worked in the Officers' Mess at the Dover Citadel barracks. He was not a great earner, and Nell took in laundry to supplement his wages. When that was still not enough, she resorted to the pawnshop, exchanging at times the children's clothes and even blankets from the beds for a few extra shillings. Alice sent her sister one pound a month to cover Ella's keep but that went towards the ten shillings a week rent that Nell struggled to pay. My mother did all she could to help, often staying away from school to look after her younger cousins while Nell went out to work. Ella, who had received barely any education, was twelve before she could proudly write her name, which she did in the frontispiece of her Bible.

A scraggy twelve-year-old, bright and cheerful, Ella made remarkable progress at school in Dover. One day, her schoolteacher announced to the class that there was a test known as the Labour Examination. Children who passed it were allowed to leave school before they were fourteen. Ella was determined to pass so she could start contributing money to the household, and to everyone's astonishment she did. On getting the result she ran home to look in the Jobs Vacant column of the *Dover Express*. She immediately got work as a housemaid for two shillings and sixpence a week – scrubbing and cleaning from seven in the morning until five in the afternoon. She was proud to be helping Nell pay the bills. She soon realised, however, that other jobs paid more and applied for a post at the town Woolworth's. Thanks to her engaging, open way, she was taken on at eight shillings a week. It was easier work and the extra money made a huge difference to the household budget, but it came to a sudden, dramatic end. The store manager sent her to get some boxes of nails from the back. He thought she was taking too long for the chore and came to chivvy her, shouting and swearing. Ella put up with a lot, but not that day – she threw the nails at him. She was sacked on the spot. Nell took the bad news with good grace and said Ella could stay home to help with the laundry. It was the autumn of 1913.

The following August, one day soon after the outbreak of the First World War, George arrived home early from work to announce he had decided to join the army. As Nell wept, he told her that if anything happened to him the army would look after her and the children – and off he went to enlist with the Royal West Surrey Regiment, the Queen's Royal Regiment (2nd of Foot), to which I was to be attached at the start of my national service in 1946. In due course the dreaded envelope arrived announcing that Sergeant George Rawlings was missing, believed killed. He died during the regiment's heroic defence of Hill 60 in April 1915. Nell was alone with five children to support.

Her son Charlie left school to work in a butcher's shop. One of his tasks was to take meat up to the Officers' Mess at the Duke of York's School. When Charlie told the chef his mother's sad story, he filled the boy's basket with food and continued to do this each week for Nell. Finally, she invited her kindly knight down to tea. They became great friends and the children loved him. His name was Chris Brown and eventually he moved in – to stay until he died, some forty years later.

Ella, meanwhile, was as usual feeling the need to play her part, to 'do her bit'. Posters about town proclaimed; 'Women, the Army needs You!'

At just under fourteen, she called at the army recruiting office. She filled in an application form, putting her age as sixteen. The woman in charge was not taken in. Declaring that Ella was certainly not sixteen, she nevertheless accepted the form and wished her luck for her cheek. Soon after, she received an official notice to report to London together with a travel pass. On arriving at Victoria Station, she saw a girl from her street named Rosie who was heading for the same address in the Bayswater Road. They asked a man for directions and when they proudly told him they were going to join the army, he exclaimed; 'Gawd 'elp England!'

Asked at the interview if she was willing to serve anywhere, Ella touchingly replied that she had to stay in Dover. When told that might not be possible, she upped and headed back home. Aunt Nell was greatly relieved to see her and in typical Macawberish-style said; 'Don't you worry, luv. Something will turn up.'

Meanwhile, Alice had written with the news that she was to marry a postman named William Waller. They were setting up home in a tenement house on Walton Street, in Chelsea. She added, also, that as Ella was now old enough to leave school and earn a living she would no longer be sending the pound a month. Nell had never told her when Ella left school two years previously.

Alice, of course, showed little motherly love for her daughter. At times, she was unfeeling to the point of cruelty. A gold bracelet, cross and chain were given to Alice for Ella by the Empress Eugénie, widow of Napoleon III of France. A Spanish countess, Eugénie de Montijo had married the headstrong son of Louis Bonaparte in 1853 and became involved in some of the most important political and military episodes in the nineteenth century. She had sought refuge in England in 1870 after the humiliating defeat of the French Army by Prussia and was joined by her husband the following year. He died in 1873. Elegant and beautiful, Eugénie, who lived until 1920, had a fine mansion built at Farnborough Hill and entertained there in imperial style. On special occasions, she employed my grandmother to cook for her and her guests. On one such occasion, she noticed that Alice was wearing mourning black and learned that it was in memory of her brother who had died in the Boer War. Eugénie recalled sadly that her only child, the Prince Imperial, had also died in Africa while serving with the British Army – killed in a skirmish with Zulu warriors in 1879. The deaths of their loved ones created a bond between the two women and when Eugénie learned that Alice had a young daughter, she presented the valuable jewellery for the child. Ella was shown it but was told by Alice that she could not wear it until she was older.

In August 1914, Alice took Ella to meet her orphaned cousin Florrie who was very sick with influenza in hospital. Florrie had been well educated. She was pretty too and spoke with a 'nice' accent. Alice thought a lot of her and told Ella that, compared to Florrie, she was stupid and plain. At the hospital, Ella was dismayed to see her cousin wearing the gold chain and bracelet she had been told were hers. Later she challenged her mother about this only to be told that the jewellery had been given to Florrie because Alice loved her, was proud of her, and because she was pretty she could wear such things – unlike Ella. Her mother's words stung like a whip on the fourteen-year-old child, who cried that she wanted to go back to Aunt Nell in Dover. Alice returned her the next day and rowed bitterly with Nell about the incident.

Ella was still keen to join up. Her opportunity to do so and yet remain in Dover came with the formation of the Women's Royal Naval Service in 1916. Lying once more about her age, she was accepted for the WRNS and served with them in Dover until the war was done. In the service, she became smart and tidy and learned to take care of officers' clothes. On leaving the WRNS, she managed to put her new skills to good use by getting work as a lady's maid in a Knightsbridge club, not far from her mother's flat in Walton Street. Alice, meanwhile, had been taken on as cook by Caroline Offley Shore – Lina.

In 1923 Lina asked Alice (now known as Mrs Waller) if she could recommend a suitable young woman to accompany her at short notice as lady's maid on a visit to France. Alice replied at first that no, she could not think of anyone. 'But what about your daughter?' Lina persisted.

Alice did her best to dissuade her, but Lina insisted and an interview was scheduled.

Ella was pleased to fill the post – and she was right to be. It was a turning point in her life and one that would have an important effect on mine. She was told to meet Lina at the barrier for the *Golden Arrow* at Victoria Station, ready to board for Paris. When she arrived, Lina informed her that because of her wartime service she would call her 'Wren'. And by that name was she known to the international high society 'liner set' that she would come to meet over the next five years.

Ella also came to know Lina's family. Her mother Emma was the youngest daughter of George Rosengarten, a German Jew who had moved to Philadelphia at the age of eighteen. There, he set up a successful pharmaceutical business. She built on the family fortune by marrying the well-to-do Charles Sinnickson and the wealthy couple set up home in Philadelphia's smart Rittenhouse Square. Thanks to the wealth and contacts of her family in America and Europe, young Lina enjoyed a fabulous social life on both sides of the Atlantic. When in London she usually stayed at the Hyde Park Hotel – and that is where I first met her in the early 1930s.

After marrying Offley Shore, she spent three years with him in India from 1909 to 1912. Partly due to his Indian empire background, she became a close friend of the Aga Khan, leader of the Ismaili Muslims and revered by them as being descended directly from the prophet Mohammed. Lina would meet up with his party in Paris or the South of France. His son, Prince Aly Khan, was half Italian, half Persian. A successful investor, the Aga Khan had boosted the family fortunes and lived in great luxury. His followers had the custom of weighing him in jewels, which he then got to keep.

Aly's father regarded him as something of a problem child. Ella befriended him, helping him with his homework despite her own lack of schooling. Lina usually stayed at The Crillon Hotel in Paris when the Aga Khan was also in residence there. In return for Ella's assistance, the young Aly would take her out on the town, the two of them leaving the hotel at night via a fire escape ('shimmying down a drain pipe', as Ella would put it) – all unbeknown to Lina. Until 1907 the hotel, standing on the Place de la Concorde, had been the Paris home of the aristocratic Crillon family. Built by order of King Louis XV in 1758, many suites were furnished in the style of his period with magnificent chandeliers and Aubusson carpets.

On one of Ella's nocturnal excursions from the hotel, she met up with a handsome Englishman who owned a successful tailoring shop in Paris. On Sundays he played the organ at the English church. In due course, he let on that he nurtured the hope Ella might marry him. Aly Khan became a great ladies' man. His second wife was to be the glamorous Hollywood screen star Rita Hayworth. In view of Aly's lifestyle, his father determined that he would not succeed him as Aga Khan – the title went to Aly's son, Karim. As a memento of their friendship, Aly gave my mother a parasol with a real rose perfectly preserved in the crystal glass ball of the handle.

Marital problems were not unusual in the family. My mother recalled that to her knowledge, in the mid-1920s, Aly's father had an affair with his wife's personal maid, who was well rewarded for her favours. In January 2012 it was reported that the fourth Aga Khan, the seventy-five-year-old Prince Karim, had been ordered by a French court to pay £50 million to his second wife as he was preparing to marry his third. However, to the head of a twelve million-strong tithe-paying community, enjoying an estimated £8 billion personal fortune, this was not a crippling sum and considerably less than the £166 million his former pop singer wife asked for when they split in 2004.

Ella's travels with Lina took her to Italy. Later she would

recall how, on her first visit, she had been appalled by the widespread poverty in the cities. Women and children would beg persistently on the steps of the churches. During a visit to Naples, Ella was disgusted when, as they left the luxurious Excelsior Hotel, Lina tried to haggle with a ragged little girl over the price of a bunch of Parma violets. She urged Lina to pay up, thrown back suddenly as she was to her own miserable childhood experience of selling oranges on the street. Unaware of the brutality of the fascist regime following Mussolini's violent takeover of the country in 1922, she would describe admiringly how by 1927 the Italian people appeared to have more pride – and, of course, how the trains ran on time. On another occasion an Italian suitor revealed how Ella had failed to keep up with the news; he asked if she would like to see 'the Great Caruso' and she said yes, delighted. On the appointed day they drove for hours into the Italian countryside, finally stopping at a fine house where a mass of people waited for admission. Puzzled, Ella joined them to wait, only realising when they filed into a room with an open casket that the world-famous tenor had kicked the bucket.

Lina loved the South of France and often stayed in Nice. The city was much favoured by wealthy Americans, such as the Vanderbilts. Ella would recall wheeling baby Gloria in her pram along the city's fashionable seafront. They also travelled to Spain and North Africa and went back and forth to America on the great liners to visit Lina's family in Philadelphia. In the basement of the family house in Rittenhouse Square, a distillery was installed to provide booze during the prohibition years. One regular visitor was the local chief of police, who would appear flagon in hand, ready to fill up.

Lina, well aware that liquor had been banned in the USA, bought twelve miniature bottles of whiskey in London to give as Christmas gifts to her father's servants in Philly. She asked

Ella to carry them. Knowing that the customs officers searched trunks and cases for contraband, Ella wrapped them in a neat parcel and carried it as hand luggage. Once on board, she placed it in a rack over her hand basin. The officers came in to search the cabin, picking it up for a heart-stopping moment before replacing it, unopened. On hearing of this, Lina laughed and later cheekily asked an officer if many were apprehended smuggling booze. 'No one slips through our fingers,' came the smug reply.

It was on that same visit that Lina, through her friendship with a well-connected English couple, was invited to stay at the British Embassy in Washington by the then Ambassador, Lord Lothian. She and Ella spent four enjoyable days there. To top that experience they were then invited for a weekend at the White House – although while President Coolidge was not in residence. Not many booze smugglers enjoyed that privileged reward!

In New York City, Ella attended the premiere of *The Jazz Singer* – the programme was one of the many things committed to her safekeeping that Alice gave or threw away. On one of Ella's last visits to Paris, Lina encouraged her to go to the airport to await the arrival of the handsome young hero, Charles Lindbergh, who was making the first ever non-stop solo flight across the Atlantic from New York. When the twenty-five-year-old aviator landed his plane, *The Spirit of St Louis*, on an airfield outside the French capital, he had not slept for sixty-three hours, having at times flown low over the waves so that the sea spray might keep him awake. Lina knew the Lindbergh family. She also knew well the American ambassador to Paris whose daughter Anne Morrow would marry the young hero two years later. The kidnapping of their baby was one of the great stories of the age.

By 1927, Lina had decided not to travel so much and

informed Ella that she would not be requiring her services as a lady's maid to anything like the same extent. Ella had to find new work. With a glowing reference from her former employer, she soon got a job in a smart residential club in Knightsbridge. There one evening she met a young man who was serving the drinks at a party. His name was Frederick Butler. He was twenty years old, good-looking and in service as an under-footman with the Clifton-Brown family. Ella, six years older, vivacious and experienced, had no boyfriend in London – although she was still considering the offer of marriage from the ex-pat tailor in Paris. She agreed to meet Frederick again. One thing led to another until, just as her mother before her, to her surprise and, one can only imagine, dismay, she was told she was pregnant. In the early summer of 1928, I was on the way.

My mother, I suppose, was a product of the Jazz Age – that period defined by its chronicler F. Scott Fitzgerald as the decade from 1919 when those who were adolescent in the First World War suddenly danced into the limelight. It was, as he wrote, the generation whose girls dramatised themselves as 'flappers'. Mother was a flapper, in short skirt or long, taking part in what Fitzgerald described as 'the greatest, gaudiest spree in history'. Thanks to Lina, my mother had enjoyed the best of it in England, France and America.

Born on 20 January 1929, I had been conceived in the dying days of that age – I had jazz in my blood. Ella and Frederick had made me legitimate by marrying the previous August, their days of 'making whoopee' ending as they settled down to a new life. Ten months after my birth, Fitzgerald's fast and fabulous era of excess, with its flaunting of sex on a tide of music and dancing, was to come to an end with the Wall Street Crash of 1929.

In England, the Labour Party won power for the second

time in a May general election – but only as a minority government. Within six months, the stock market slide quickly spread economic depression to London and other financial centres around the world. By June 1930, unemployment in Britain had risen to 1.9 million and by the end of the year it hit 2.5 million. Without the support of a welfare state, families faced the humiliation of the means test. It was a worrying time for my father.

My father's employer, the decent Colonel Clifton-Brown, was to become Speaker of the House of Commons. He accepted that the young man could no longer continue 'living in' as a low-paid under-footman and needed a new job that allowed him to be at home with his wife and child. Helpfully, he arranged for him to become a messenger at the Anglo-American Brown Shipley Bank in the city – a bank with which the Clifton-Brown family had a strong connection. It was also the institution with which Lina banked. Frederick would start at a wage of under £3 a week, an average working class income at the time. Some sixty years later, Ella was invited to the bank to identify a gold tea service thought to belong to Lina, found forgotten in a safety deposit box.

As for a home for the newly-weds, grandmother Alice made up – somewhat – for her past neglect by offering my parents her small basement flat at 33 Walton Street. She had made little use of it since the death of her 'husband' (we were never quite convinced he did make an honest woman of her), William Waller.

Brown Shipley was a good employer and continued to take a caring interest in the welfare of my parents after my father was obliged to retire early on medical advice in 1958. His chain-smoking habit had severely damaged his lungs and he was advised to move out of London in search of cleaner air in the country. My parents found it in the village of West

Hougham, mid-way between Folkestone and Aunt Nell's family in Dover. There, with mother's nest egg, they bought a rose-covered cottage a few miles inland from the white cliffs. My father's ill-judged gambling and generosity had not been conducive to saving. Apart from his bank pension, he received a Christmas bonus and payments for health care. After he died, at the age of 67, my mother was awarded his pension. She also got a Christmas hamper and private hospital treatment. The bank appeared to me to exemplify solid City success, a much respected, gentlemanly financial institution enjoying the highest influence. My father admired his employers, explaining to me that in their circles 'their word was their bond'. Influenced by him, I naively grew up to believe that all merchant bankers were true gentlemen. I was to learn the hard way that this was not so.

Soon after my mother's death I read a report in *The Times* on June 26th, 1992, recording 'Brown Shipley, one of the City's oldest merchant banks, has been sold to a Luxembourg bank for the princely sum of £1'. The reporter, Jon Ashworth, went on to explain that, after nearly two hundred years, the sale had removed from City control one of the best-known names in British merchant banking. Sir Edward Heath had once worked there and Montagu Norman, a partner before the Great War, had gone on to become the longest-serving Governor of the Bank of England, from 1920-44. Ashworth noted that some City boys were suggesting the Luxemburghers had been fleeced, as £1 seemed a steep price for the banking arm of a group that had just revealed a pre-tax loss of £27.1 million.

Edward Heath's youthful stint as a hand-picked trainee at the bank had brought him into contact with my father, one of whose responsibilities was to organise the directors' lunches and drinks parties. This link proved helpful to me when, as Lobby Correspondent for the *News Chronicle* at the House of

Commons, I needed to introduce myself to him, then Chief Whip of the Tory Party. He was immediately friendly. Later we would lunch together, I entertaining him at the Savoy Hotel's famous Grill Room and he returning my hospitality by inviting me to dine at his tastefully furnished, manly apartment at Albany, off Piccadilly. Like my father, I grew to respect him.

2

Soldier Mad

My first memory is of sitting in a pram while sunshine filtered first through the iron railings at street level and next through the net curtains at a window behind me. My father entered through a door on the other side of the gas-lit room. I was in our living and dining quarters that, together with one bedroom and a small scullery, made up our Chelsea basement home. There was no bathroom and a lavatory on a landing above was shared with all the tenants on the first floor. There was no running hot water. Instead it was heated in a kettle or saucepan on the small gas cooker in the scullery. Bathing was a palaver. The flat was damp. How Mother must have missed the Crillon!

By the time I was three, I was diagnosed with rheumatism and my parents decided that a move to less damp and pokey quarters was required. They found another flat in a block along the road – Marlborough Buildings. It was still a basement but did not appear to be damp. It was larger and we had a loo of our own! Our neighbours included postmen, policemen, waiters and widows.

Walton Street was very different then from the smart thoroughfare of chi-chi restaurants, boutiques, antique shops and interior decorators it has become. It catered to the working class. There was a Welsh dairy run by 'Dai the Milk', scrupulous in his cleanliness; a newsagent; a greengrocer; a butcher; a baker; and halfway along, a GP's surgery. There, my mother was told that at the age of four I now had rheumatism in my back – 'like an old man'. The doctor suggested we move out of the basement. Luckily, an upstairs flat became available soon afterwards and we levitated up into the light.

At four years old, I was enrolled in the infant section of Marlborough School in Draycott Avenue. The teachers were impressed by my painting and drawing. When I was six, they entered one of my watercolours in an exhibition of local children's art at Chelsea Town Hall. It depicted a frenetic jazz band, inspired by a performance of Louis 'Satchmo' Armstrong and his men that I had seen in *Pennies from Heaven*, a film that had me singing down the Kings Road with an umbrella upside down. I would remain a fan of Armstrong's for the rest of my life. Eight decades later, my daughter brought me souvenirs from his house in Queens, New York. The art on King Louis' walls included a crucifixion scene by Salvador Dali. The guide allegedly maintained that Louis would wake up each morning, stretch and salute the canvas with 'Well, hello Dali'. One can only wish it true.

At home, I spent hour upon hour drawing and painting. When I was done with that I would play with my fast-growing collection of lead soldiers. From when I could first walk and talk, I was enthralled by men in military-style dress. I would shout 'Soljar! Soljar!' excitedly at anyone in uniform, from telegraph boys to our local Chelsea Pensioners. Despite my fascination – or perhaps because of it – my mother lost no opportunity to talk about the horrors of the First World War.

Dover had been a front line town, regularly bombed and shelled and full of troops and naval personnel. She recounted stories of the appalling miseries of life in the trenches that she had heard from soldiers on leave or from the wounded, often terribly mutilated, men who were disembarked at the docks. My father, being six years younger, and brought up in the historic Kent country town of Faversham, could not compete with such stories and was not influenced by the carnage and devastation of the conflict. He was one of the youngest of a large family that had a happy, loving existence, even though money was always short in their small terraced house. His father did a number of low-paid labouring jobs, keeping rabbits and an allotment to supplement the family table. As soon as he was old enough, my father did his bit by raiding the orchards surrounding the town, running home with an abundance of apples, pears and plums. In the winter he would raid coal dumps near the local railway station to keep the home fire burning.

At school he did well in lessons and his report card also noted his neatness and skill at drawing. When the time came to leave, he earned money as an errand boy before following one of his older sisters into service, taking a position as an under-footman. His appearance helped him to get the job. He was slim, and looked smart in uniform. At first he spent much of his time doing chores for more senior members of the staff as well as the work required for his employers. Accordingly he was one of the first up in the morning, helping to prepare breakfast for the staff, lighting fires and pressing the day's copy of *The Times* with an iron before it was taken up to the master of the house. He would then be polishing shoes and boots or brushing and pressing outdoor clothes. He was also employed in running messages, dusting the silver and cleaning glass. On occasions when the family had guests for lunch or dinner he would assist the butler, wearing his best uniform.

Father's natural conservatism was reinforced by his experience in service and his later employment in the Brown Shipley Bank. My mother's life and nature, on the other hand, ensured that she would support the growing Labour Movement. Occasionally I witnessed political arguments at home, sparked by an item in our daily newspaper. Father bought the *Daily Express*, although Mother would have preferred the Labour-orientated *Daily Herald*. My favourite part of the paper – even before Rupert Bear – was what I called 'the funny page'. It contained the daily political cartoon. The issues were beyond my understanding but I delighted in the caricatures of politicians of the day – Lloyd George, Churchill, Ramsay MacDonald, Baldwin and Chamberlain. On the international scene there were drawings of the dictators – Hitler, Mussolini and Franco, and, fighting for India's independence, the scrawny, saintly Gandhi, dressed in what looked to me like an old bed sheet.

My favourite cartoonist was the gifted David Low, who for twenty-three years drew his corrosive caricatures for Lord Beaverbrook's *Evening Standard*. The mischievous Canadian peer gave the socialist Low a free hand to lampoon politicians of all parties and foreign statesmen – his cartoons aimed at Hitler and Mussolini gave rise to protests from the sensitive fascist dictators. Attempts to suppress them by top people in Whitehall, anxious to keep the peace with aggressive tyrants, were rightly ignored by *The Beaver*. My favourite Low character was Colonel Blimp, an overweight, reactionary conservative, who spent much of his time fulminating in Turkish baths.

Politics took on a more serious tone when, for our summer hols sometime in the 1930s, we visited Aunt Nell in Dover. By now, the kindly Chris had become her husband and two of her sons, George and Alfred, were miners in the Kent coalfield. This was a pit known for militancy. Unmarried, the two men still lived with Nell in the cramped terraced house. The square table that dominated the small living room always seemed set for a meal, thanks to the shift system they worked.

The failure of the 1926 General Strike – precipitated by an

attempt to reduce miners' wages – still cast a shadow over Nell's household. More than 162 million working days had been lost due to that strike action, 146 million of those in the coal industry. After all their sacrifices, the miners felt bitterly that they had been let down by the TUC. Following the collapse of the strike the coal owners, in vengeful mood, moved in against their workers, imposing wage cuts on those who had not been sacked.

As hundreds of banks collapsed in the economic turmoil of the 1930s depression, my father feared for his own job. As a new boy in his early twenties at the Brown Shipley Bank, he assumed that if staff cuts were required he would go – 'last in, first out'. The bank, however, survived. Hardest hit were the labour intensive industries. The dithering minority Labour Government under Ramsay MacDonald came under increasing pressure from the militant Miners' Federation and from distinguished economists such as Maynard Keynes. They called for intervention as the jobless total climbed to well over two million – a rate approaching fifteen per cent of Britain's population of some forty-six million.

The coalfields were an appalling scene of worsening deprivation and poverty. MacDonald's desperate decision in August 1931 to form a national government was an attempt to solve the economic crisis. Instead, it split the Labour Party and in the general election that autumn Labour was left with only fifty-two MPs, of whom twenty-three were sponsored by the Miners' Federation. The new government's punitive economic measures did little to revive the economy and by the end of the year nearly three million were out of work. Benefits were cut by ten per cent, regulations governing entitlements were tightened and a humiliating means test placed a twenty-six week limit on 'the dole'. Once that was up, those claiming relief had their situations examined by Public Assistance Committees. Nearly a million unemployed were subjected to the hated means test by early 1932 – receiving visits from seemingly unsympathetic 'relieving officers' who entered their homes and checked their possessions. Aunt Nell had experienced similarly intrusive relief visits when she sought assistance after her first husband's death in action during the First World War.

In 1935, a new battle loomed over a wage rise that became known as the 'Miners' Two Bob'. The talk around Nell's table became increasingly hostile to the established order. So it was that when Edward, Prince of Wales, visiting destitute Welsh mining communities, declared in horror and frustration that 'something must be done', Nell and her family believed with relief that at last something would indeed be done. Their hope of some initiative from the top even increased briefly when the Prince was proclaimed King on the death of George V in January 1936. Although my mother had told them about his affair with Mrs Simpson, they did not realise that she would be more important to the new King than his people.

It was revealed only in January 2012 that during the abdication crisis a member of MI5 in London tapped private conversations between Edward VIII and his brother, the Duke of York. This must be one of the earliest recorded incidents of phone hacking and was carried out on the orders of Prime Minister Stanley Baldwin in a desperate attempt to keep abreast of the careering developments. Politicians, then, had their hands in this game before the press, much as they have occupied the moral high ground lately at the Leveson Enquiry. The arras behind which the sneaky civil servant lurked was a telephone junction box close to the Duke's home at 145 Piccadilly – but I failed to spot him from the top deck of the bus.

Just as the crisis over Edward and Mrs Simpson was reaching its peak and threatening to topple the monarchy, I witnessed the collapse of another of London's great edifices. In the public's mind, the Crystal Palace was very much linked to the royal family, being as it was the enclosure and symbol of the Great Exhibition of 1851, brainchild of Queen Victoria's creative consort Prince Albert. This had been moved from its original site in Hyde Park to sit atop a hill in South London, where it gave its name to the surrounding environs. On the first day of December 1936, the house of glass caught fire. During the summer my parents had taken me to see it on a day out, but now my father led me out to our back yard to see the calamitous red glow in the cold night sky – such as the Luftwaffe would recreate in just a few years' time.

I was taken to see another solemn event; the funeral procession for George V and his lying-in-state in the Great Hall at the Palace of Westminster. He and Queen Mary had seemed popular with the people around me. Many years later, however, a member of the royal household – the irrepressible William Tallon – revealed to me just how indifferent, if not brutal, the King could be to low-ranking servants. Fly fishing in Scotland, and watched by members of the family, the King's hook caught a gillie in the face. The injured man fell, as members of the royal party clustered around him. 'You've taken out his eye!' exclaimed one horrified onlooker, running up to the monarch who had continued with his fishing.

'He's got another one, hasn't he?' retorted King George, allegedly, with some impatience.

As for Queen Mary, the aristocracy greeted the announcement of an impending visit by Her Majesty with some horror for she was a notorious 'collector' of valuable antiques from the great houses of England. The finest jade and porcelain graced her tables and shelves – much of it handed over to her reluctantly by hosts all over the empire.

Attending a reception in the 1980s at Marlborough House, once home to the old Queen, I learned more about her collecting habit from the Earl of Shannon. Her MO was to visit regularly the stately piles known to have fine collections. There, she would admire certain items so pointedly that her hosts felt obliged to offer them as a memento of her stay. One member of the aristocracy who had been plundered once too often went to extraordinary lengths to keep the rapacious Queen at bay. This Scottish lord paid a member of her household £100 a year to phone him as soon as Her Majesty was heading for Scotland. By the time she had arrived for a 'surprise' call on his estate, shutters were drawn and every indication given to support the servants' apologetic explanation that the family was not at home. After the old Queen's death, her son George VI is supposed to have returned many items that had been 'donated' to his magpie mother's collection.

More welcome guests, my grandparents, came up from Faversham to stay with us to view the magnificent coronation procession of King George VI. This shy, decent, dedicated man had been proclaimed monarch by default, on the abdication of his feckless brother. Members of the court circle, the real aristocracy and the government were relieved when Edward departed. One of Lina's palace informants was Sir Clive (later Lord) Wigram. He had been Private Secretary to George V for many years after leaving the Indian Army, where he had been a friend of General Offley Shore. Lina told my mother that Sir Clive had been deeply worried by Prince Edward's behaviour – not least his womanising – and had resolved to retire from his post after the death of the old King.

On Coronation Day, my father shepherded our little party to Park Lane. There, we took up our positions to watch the procession. People already camped along the route kindly allowed my pipsqueak self to get to the front for a better view. As the infantry and cavalry regiments swept by in a glittering flood of military splendour, I remember being most impressed by the Indian Army contingent. My dedication to the superb turbaned horsemen was to be given a further boost soon after by a film entitled *Lives of a Bengal Lancer*, starring Gary Cooper and Franchot Tone. I saw it several times over the years – as did an unlikely fan in Germany. Adolf Hitler was so taken with the way the British conducted themselves in the film during their dealings with their Indian subjects that he instructed his officers to watch and learn from it regarding being a worthy master race. My mother was another great fan of the flicks. Every week she would meet me from school with a bag of homemade cakes and then we would walk together to the Kings Road nearby to catch the latest film. In the cinema there I was introduced to the magical team of Fred Astaire and Ginger Rogers in films like *The Gay Divorcee* and *Top Hat*. Munching cakes, I watched transfixed as they glided through breathtaking routines to such numbers as Cole Porter's 'Night and Day'. On other visits, I brushed up my history with films about Clive of India or the Iron Duke of Wellington. For Mother, the cinema provided an escape from penny-pinching real life in our small flat. In front of the silver screen, she could return to the glamour of her travels with Lina for a couple of hours.

Our visits to the cinema usually coincided with my father's part-time work as a waiter at dinners and receptions for a City Livery Company or the Corporation of London. He had built a reputation as one of the most reliable and polished waiters in London and supplemented his small wage from the bank with his evening earnings. Unfortunately, he was also both an unlucky gambler and a generous man. Most of his extra earnings were lost on the horses or dogs. On the rare occasion that he did win, he would treat Mother and me to an outing, and his friends to drinks – leaving little or nothing to put in the bank. Fortunately, when we needed money, my grandmother Alice helped out.

Since 1928 Alice had been working as resident cook for Lina, who occupied the drawing room floor flat at fashionable 49 Grosvenor Square. In the early 1930s, Mother took me each week to visit her for tea in the spacious kitchen. Invariably I would be summoned for an interview with Lina, whom I had been trained to address as 'Madam'. She had greatly wanted a child of her own but married late and, while in India, suffered a miscarriage. Having no son, she made a great fuss of me. From her, I received my first box of lead soldiers. They came from Harrods. She told me about Offley's army career. He had passed out from the Royal Military Academy, Sandhurst, and said that if, in due course, I wanted to go there too she would help me. I was fascinated by her stories of Offley's life in the Indian Army, where he became Quartermaster-General in charge of training. He was stationed in the pleasant hill town of Simla. One of my favourite teatime accounts was of their attendance at the 1911 Delhi Durbar, a great military spectacle in honour of George V, the new Emperor of India. The native chiefs' procession took one and a half hours to pass and included every style of uniform and combination of colours. Horsemen wearing ancient chain armour were mounted on horses that walked on hind legs. In all, there were some 60,000 troops on parade.

Inspired by her descriptions, I painted my own version of the Durbah and presented it on my next visit. She was touched and told how the General had been a gifted artist, promising to show me some of his drawings of life in India. On birthdays and at Christmas she would send me money (to buy soldiers!) and always wrote a newsy letter, at the end writing sideways across her own writing to avoid having to use another sheet of paper. I found these last lines very difficult to read, but apparently this was her normal custom when corresponding. 'That's how people become millionaires – saving on notepaper', explained my mother.

With Edward's abdication, he became the Duke of Windsor and the Princesses were installed at the palace. At the coronation of their parents in 1937, the seven-year-old Margaret asked her elder sister why their Uncle David, as they knew him, was not present at the function. 'He abdicated', Elizabeth replied.

'Why?' asked Margaret Rose.

'He wanted to marry Mrs Baldwin', explained the future Queen, with some confused authority. She had heard Prime Minister Baldwin's name mentioned in connection with the crisis.

Sometimes, if we did not travel by bus to see my grandmother, we would walk through Hyde Park. On one occasion I brought my toy yacht to sail on the Serpentine. I let the string slip from my fingers and the yacht began to drift from the shore. My mother bent down to retrieve it and I was suddenly overcome by a great temptation. I gave her a little push and she tottered in her high heels into the lake. As she staggered dripping out of the water I feared for a moment that she would do me a serious injury. She had a frightening temper. Faced with a sizeable audience of lakeside strollers, however, she made do with giving me a sharp slap on the legs before dragging me away.

Photographs of Mother taken on her travels in the mid-twenties reveal her as a fashionable flapper, often in a cloche hat. In the 1930s, her language continued to be spattered with catchphrases from that 'roaring' era, such as 'the bee's knees' or 'the cat's pyjamas'. She also used odd foreign-sounding phrases such as 'san fairy Anne', which I later figured out derived from the French *ca ne fait rien* – 'that doesn't matter'. As she bustled around at her housework she was always singing – sometimes songs from the First World War; sometimes anglicised versions of French and Italian songs; sometimes numbers from comic opera and music hall. In my grandmother's flat stood a large cabinet gramophone and among her records was one of Master Ernest Lough, a fifteen-year-old chorister of the Temple Church Choir, singing 'O for the Wings of a Dove'. Made in 1927, it was one of the most popular classical records for some decades, selling over a million copies. One of my grandmother's favourite recordings was the German tenor Richard Tauber singing 'You Are My Heart's Delight' – another big hit of the day. As for my own efforts in the choir of St Saviours, I had a reputation for giggling so the other junior choristers would pull faces at me during the services and concerts to start me off and annoy the choirmaster.

Mother did her best to bring a note of culture into our little home. By collecting coupons from newspapers and other sources, she filled a shelf with the full set of Charles Dickens' novels and was able to hang several pictures on the walls including a reproduction of *Mother and Son* by the artist Henry William Banks Davis – a painting of a white mare with her chestnut foal of which Stubbs could have been proud.

At some time in her younger days, Mother had been introduced to the poem *If* by Rudyard Kipling. It impressed her and when I was eight years old, she bought a framed copy and hung it by my bed – to provide some guidance. I liked the ringing last lines:

> If you can fill the unforgiving minute
> With sixty seconds' worth of distance run,
> Yours is the earth and everything that's in it,
> And – which is more – you'll be a man, my son!

When we had guests, Mother would invariably turn the conversation to her travels, showing postcards of cities she had visited. At school, I would surprise my teachers by describing such sights as Vesuvius overlooking the Bay of Naples and by painting pictures of them. Prince Aly Khan had taken Mother to the top of the live volcano. Lina had gone to Naples to join a party being hosted by his father the Aga Khan. Prince Aly had arranged to take two of the lady guests to view the famous crater, but at the last minute they had let him down. He offered to take Mother and another lady's maid instead. Up they went and for his party piece, their guide dropped a coin into a puddle of molten lava. When it had hardened he presented it to my mother, who had it on display for the rest of her life along with little bits of souvenir china, meticulously dusted; dolls in various national dress kept immaculate in a glass cabinet; and shoe boxes full of frilly-edged photographs of her extraordinary excursions. Such travel experiences were rare in the 1930s for people of our class. I was determined that one day I would see such places for myself.

Overhanging us, however, was the shadow of the general industrial depression. With so many out of work there was the fear that my father, too, might become unemployed. Mother was haunted by memories of the means test humiliation suffered by Aunt Nell and memories of her appalling early childhood. She swore that if she and my father – for any reason – could not look after me, they would never send me to live with another family. Instead, I would be sent to an institution, such as a Barnardo's Home – and a Barnardo's saving box shaped like a cottage stood in our living room. I was encouraged to put in part of any money given to me.

Despite our move to an upstairs flat, my health was not robust and my parents began to consider moving out of central London with its pea-soup fogs and smoky pollution. Eventually, in 1938, we did – to a semi-detached pebble-dashed house in Fairholme Avenue, Gidea Park. On the outskirts of Romford, a busy market town in Essex, Gidea Park had been named and developed as a showcase housing development in 1910. The site was known as Romford Garden Suburb and received its name from the nearby Elizabethan mansion, Gidea Hall. The houses had sold quickly, helped by the fact that a Gidea Park railway station had been opened, providing a fast link to the city. A golf course had been added too.

There was no question of us buying the property. My grandmother helped out with the rent. Like most working class families living from hand to mouth, my parents could not contemplate the risks and maintenance costs involved in home ownership. At the end of the First World War, home ownership in Britain was only about twenty-three per cent; everyone else rented. A small fraction of housing was provided by the public sector and council houses were often low grade. My parents continued to rent until they bought a retirement cottage in Kent in the early 1960s. They had at last become part of the great expansion of privately-owned housing that marked the mid-twentieth century.

The move to Gidea Park was a big step up the housing – and social – ladder for us. The house had three bedrooms, a living room, a dining room connected by a serving hatch to the kitchen – and a bathroom (our first). There was also a garden with a fishpond and space for a garage. I joined a nearby primary school and soon impressed the teachers with my artistic efforts. With new friends, I fished for newts in the pond on the golf course, cycled to Warley Woods, or hiked over fields beyond the Eastern Avenue to picnic in haystacks. It was my first experience of something approaching country life and my health steadily improved.

In the great world beyond, international relations were steadily deteriorating. Militant fascism was on the march in Italy and Nazi Germany. In the cinema, I watched Pathé newsreels of Mussolini's conquest of Ethiopia and the opening of the Spanish Civil War. In 1936, the Republican Popular Front had been elected into government in Spain, committed to revolutionary change in a country where most people lived in rural poverty. Greatly alarmed, the landowners, middle classes and churchmen supported a nationalist rebel uprising led by General Franco. Nazi Germany and Italy sided with Franco and used Spain as a testing ground for tactics and weapons. In the cinema, we witnessed the result of the bombing of Guernica. For the German bomber pilots, it was a useful trial run for raids to come elsewhere.

The Spanish Civil War split opinion in Britain – and in our family. While Conservative right-wingers supported Franco, the left backed the Republican Government. Over 500 Britons died as volunteers in the International Brigade formed to augment the hard-pressed government army. One was a friend of George, my great-cousin, in Dover. By this time, George was describing himself as a Communist and reading the *Daily Worker*. In later life, I was to get to know a number of men who fought in the Brigade and had a feeling that if I had been of their age I would have done so, too. In Fairholme Avenue, there was a flutter of interest when a Spanish family seeking refuge from the victorious fascists took up residence and a small, dark-haired boy appeared kicking a ball and looking for friends. By the time it was over in 1939, the conflict had involved appalling savagery. It became the curtain-raiser for the Second World War.

In the autumn of 1938, the Nazi rape of Czechoslovakia began with the occupation of the Sudeten areas. Neville Chamberlain, who had become Britain's Prime Minister in May 1937, then signed the infamous Munich Agreement. The final phase of the country's policy of appeasement of fascist aggression had been ushered in. I watched him on a newsreel arriving back in England after meeting with Hitler, waving his copy of the shameful agreement aloft while claiming to have achieved 'peace with honour'. He had, in fact, been faced with the choice of peace *or* honour. At home, we listened to a broadcast by the weary-sounding premier in which he complained: 'How horrible, fantastic, incredible it is that we should be digging trenches and trying on gasmasks here because of a quarrel in a far-away country between people of whom we know nothing.'

Mother, whose First World War experience had led her to support the pacifist wing of the Labour Party, was relieved that hostilities had, at least, been postponed. She described Churchill as a warmonger. Father said some people in the City were saying that Chamberlain had gained a little precious time for Britain to prepare for the inevitable conflict. In the sports field at the end of our garden, trenches were being dug. They were muddy and smelly. Father volunteered for the Auxiliary Fire Service and we applauded when he arrived home in his dark-blue uniform.

For me a more personal crisis was looming – the 'Eleven Plus' examination. Being weak at arithmetic, I was not confident. My parents, as always, refused to put pressure on me. 'Just do your best and don't worry', they advised.

My best was not good enough. I failed to win a place at the local secondary school. We were informed that there might be one at Wanstead High School, further away, subject to passing an interview. The alternative was technical school in Romford. In view of my artistic bent and inability to cope with things mechanical, that seemed hardly ideal. So I presented myself for the interview at Wanstead. It was conducted by the rather stern-looking headmaster, A.F. Joseph, an Oxford Classics MA who had served with the Indian Army in the First World War. I impressed him with my answers on literature and history, and not long afterwards my parents were informed that I was in. I had become one of the grammar school set.

My departure from Salisbury Road Elementary was not

without regrets, for I had been happy there. In my last year I had been asked to paint a mural of a medieval tournament on the corridor wall outside my classroom. It was based on a colourful, action-filled picture I had done in class. The younger children would gather around in admiration as I worked on it, a scene, as I imagined it, like the studio of a Renaissance master.

Autograph albums were something of a craze and I asked my form master, popular 'Daddy' Dicks, to write a farewell message in mine. I had two nicknames – Angel Face and Dish. A photograph of me in choirboy's surplice, stiff collar and bow tie inspired the first. The other was more oblique – Butler became 'butter dish' which in turn was shortened to 'dish'. Mr Dicks wrote;

> Whatever people call you, be it Angel Face or Dish,
> Take your bearings from heaven,
> And strive as well as wish.

The friends I left behind in Gidea Park included a clever, good-looking boy named Graham Waddup, a promising pianist. His doting mother had carefully trained a quiff of hair to curl over his forehead. Graham was embarrassed by it and we agreed it made him look like a sissy. One day, in a handicraft lesson, we were issued with scissors and he asked me to cut it off. I obliged. His mother had a holy fit when he arrived home. She blamed me for the rape of the lock – and added a few more unladylike epithets to my list of nicknames.

I had been reading the military stories by the famous Victorian author G.A. Henty. Books such as *The Young Carthaginian*, about a boy who served in Hannibal's army, improved my knowledge of history. With their elephants, they crossed the Alps to conquer Italy. I was a child of the British Empire. I enjoyed the Empire Day ceremonies each year when we assembled in the school hall, bedecked with Union Jacks, to be addressed by some local dignitary. Then someone would recite a suitably blood-stirring poem. My favourite compared a school cricket match with a regiment's last stand and ended with the incantation 'Play up, play up and play the game'. Best of all we were given a half-day holiday. No wonder the empire seemed such a 'Good Thing'.

At dawn on 1 September 1939, aircraft of the German Luftwaffe swept across the frontiers of Poland to open the blitzkrieg on that heroic country. Two days later, Chamberlain declared war on the Nazis on behalf of ill-prepared Britain. Mother looked distraught. We gathered around the radio to hear Chamberlain's uninspiring voice confirm that we were at war. To add authority to the announcement, air raid sirens began their wailing warning almost before he had finished speaking on that tense Sunday morning. We ran into the street to be shouted at by an officious local air-raid warden, so we scurried back inside. None of our neighbours seemed to be heading for those mucky trenches in the playing field. Then, soon after, the 'all clear' sounded. 'Jerry didn't waste much time', said Father, pouring himself, somewhat earlier than usual, a glass of brown ale.

Soon we learned that London schools were being evacuated to what were deemed safer areas. Wanstead High School was sent to Chippenham in Wiltshire. However, as a late addition to the school roll, I missed the Chippenham coach. Instead, with half a dozen other late additions, I found myself attached to the newly-formed Chingford County High School heading for the little town of Coleford in Gloucestershire, set in the mystical, magical Royal Forest of Dean. I had got chatting to a boy before we boarded and we sat next to each other on the coach. His name was Alan Barton and I soon discovered that, for his age – and unlike me – he knew a lot about cricket. All these years later we are still close friends. We started with one thing in common. Like me, he had needed an interview to get into the school.

In a community hall in Coleford, we were allocated our billets. 'Who'd like to live on a farm?' asked the woman in charge.

I nudged Alan, quickly put up my hand and shouted; 'We would!'

'That's all right. They can take two. You'll be going to Broadwell,' she replied.

Life was about to become very different for the two of us.

3

No Passage to India

The woman voluntary worker's car stopped at the gate of Broadwell Farm and as I peered into the yard, my heart missed a beat. There before us stood an unusual-looking man. Short, with a brown, wrinkled face, long arms, large hands and bowed legs, he was wearing a brown bowler hat, black jacket, knee breeches, leggings and boots. He was Farmer Milsom Blanch. As he opened the gate to the farmyard he called out to someone in the house behind him;

'They're here, Lil!'

Out came his wife Lillian, a strapping woman, taller than him, plain of face, with large red arms and a business-like manner.

Alan and I were bustled into a narrow kitchen, through a large, well-furnished dining room and up a flight of stairs to a good-sized bedroom with a double bed that we were to share. The window looked out on to a field and to one side was the entrance to a cowshed.

Despite his somewhat anthropoid appearance, Mr Blanch turned out to be one of the kindest, steadiest and most patient men I have ever known. The hard-working Lillian, stricter than her husband, was a straight-talking pillar of the local church determined to look after our spiritual as well as our physical needs.

Life in the house was spent mostly around the table in the kitchen where the ever-lit coal stove saw Lillian cooking and heating the water for cleaning and bathing. This was drawn by bucket from a deep well outside the front door. The WC was outside in the garden. Oil lamps and candles lit the house. The thirty-acre farm maintained a small herd of dairy cows, two large pigs in a cramped sty and a flock of wandering chickens whose eggs sometimes turned up in surprising places. At the edge of one field was a small mineshaft, where two men came daily to dig for coal. They were 'free miners' of the Forest of Dean who had the traditional right to dig for minerals within its bounds – thirty-five square miles of hilly land surrounded by the rivers Severn, Wye and Leadon. Britain's greatest oak forest, it boasts trees more than 1,000 years old and has been noted for rich deposits of coal and iron. I learned that iron had been excavated there for some 4,000 years. In the grounds of a house owned by Lillian's sister were the remains of a mine, overgrown by ferns and lichens, dating back to the Roman occupation.

For a boy of eleven, the forest was a paradise. As I clambered among the moss-covered trees and rocks, clutching for support at the tangled wild woodbine, I pictured the days when it was a hunting ground for Norman lords and knights. It was granted royal status by William the Conqueror. Two years before I arrived, it was designated a National Forest Park. All over roamed the sheep of the Forest Commoners who, since Norman times, have claimed the right to graze their flocks free of charge. The grass, as a result, was cropped into fine lawns running at some points to the edge of disused quarries. The sheep would also wander around Broadwell village eating flowerbeds and vegetable gardens, until shooed away by furious housewives.

The people of the forest had a distinct and colourful dialect. A young lad who did odd jobs around the farm taught me the basic local welcome; 'Ow bist ol' butty?' or, in London lingo; 'How are you mate?'

This, however, afforded me no protection when Alan and I confronted some village lads trespassing in one of the farm's fields. I came out of the short, sharp punch-up with a black eye.

The Chingford High evacuees and the Wanstead contingent were to use an empty infants' school near Coleford's ancient Bell's Grammar School. Some years earlier, a local girl had done well there, going on to marry up-and-coming Labour politician Denis Healey, later Chancellor of the Exchequer. We used the grammar school's laboratories, excellent playing fields and any other facilities needed for our syllabus. A boy named John Morgan, returning from being evacuated to America, joined us after term had already started. I would meet up with him again in 1948 at the London School of Economics. From there, he graduated to enjoy a successful career at the Foreign Office.

He served as Britain's ambassador to South Korea, Poland and Mexico. I was sorry to read of his death in June 2012. Our paths had crossed again in the 1970s when, as head of the FO's Cultural Relations Department, he had to take note of the highly successful Pompeii Exhibition at the Royal Academy, which I had succeeded in getting my client, the Imperial Tobacco Company, to sponsor.

Early in his career he had served as an interpreter at international conferences and interpreted for Harold Macmillan when he visited Moscow in 1959. Macmillan asked him for something to say in Russian when meeting people. Morgan suggested: *Dobry Den* ('Good day') and told him that if he said 'double gin' that would be the correct pronunciation. The Prime Minister used the phrase with much enthusiasm. To my dismay, after retiring from the Diplomatic Service with the customary knighthood, Morgan became a paid consultant to the arch rogue and swindler, Robert Maxwell, already labelled by a Board of Trade enquiry as unfit to run a public company. By then I had turned down several offers of jobs from 'Captain Bob'.

Although I had scraped into the school on interview, I came top of the class in the first term and was elected form captain. I was reading a lot and had discovered the American writer James Fenimore Cooper and his tales of the North American Indians and the intrepid frontiersmen. In my forays into the forest, I was inspired by *The Last of the Mohicans*. Come autumn we were taught rugby football, a game I quickly embraced.

Meanwhile, back in Gidea Park, my father had decided that rather than wait to be called up for the armed forces he would volunteer and so, hopefully, be allowed to choose which service he joined. He chose the RAF because even the lowest ranks wore a collar and tie. When, in due course, he informed me he had been promoted to Leading Aircraftsman I imagined he would be zooming in a Spitfire down on the enemy as he led his squadron into battle. In fact, on the strength of his experience as a footman, valet and waiter, he had ended up as a batman. And how lucky were the officers who got him as their servant.

With my father in the RAF, Mother decided to give up our house and moved into my grandmother's vacant flat in Walton Street. Lina, on the strength of General Offley Shore's loyal service, had been granted a grace and favour apartment in the Clock Tower at Hampton Court Palace. My grandmother had moved with her. Widows of distinguished servicemen had been allotted these apartments by the Crown since the eighteenth century and some were by now in dire need of modernisation. Two of Lina's neighbours were Lady Fisher, widow of the commander of the British Navy in the First World War, and Lady Baden-Powell, widow of the South African war hero and founder of the Boy Scouts movement. The Clock Tower, with its narrow, winding stairway, needed a lift to enable the elderly ladies to get from floor to floor. This was a major expense. Lina, of course, could afford to have one installed. Rather than use the new lift to collect deliveries, however, my grandmother would let down a basket from her kitchen window near the tower's archway – a habit that amused visiting tourists. When, as a young officer, I was stationed at the Ordnance Regimental Depot at nearby Feltham and visited her, she would let down the front door key in the same basket. On one of my first visits as a small boy of nine, I was taken on an improving tour of the palace. My attention was grabbed by a painting of *The Rape of the Sabine Women*. Some days after, back in Chelsea, Mother was entertaining some girlfriends for tea while I sat engrossed with my paint box. 'What are you painting there, Arthur?' asked one of the guests.

I held up my representation of ample-bosomed women, togas asunder, being chased across the street by lusty Romans to shocked silence. My mother grabbed the paper, gasping 'I think it's time you put your paints away!'

On her own in Chelsea, my mother got work as a waitress in the restaurant of Selfridges store in Oxford Street. There, she served through the devastating German bombing raids of the Blitz, often walking to work along roads covered in broken glass and debris.

Women staff members of Selfridges were not allowed to use their married names and Ella was re-named 'Miss Bedway'. My father was not pleased, fearing that male customers would assume my attractive mother was a free and easy single woman. He should have been glad her store name was not Miss Bedworthy!

Soon after its opening in 1909, some enterprising manager from the department store stopped my grandmother on Oxford

Street and invited her to pose in a window brushing her lovely long hair. She did not get to meet Harry Selfridge himself, but he took a great interest in his window displays and promotions, as was depicted in the dramatised television series of early 2013 about his colourful life. He virtually invented the art of window dressing and inspected them every day. He clearly approved of my grandmother advertising his products. Those were the high days.

By the time my mother dealt with him in 1941 Harry was a ruined man. Apart from extravagant store promotions, the American tycoon squandered huge sums on gambling and mistresses. The high-living merchant was voted off the board of the store that bore his name. Virtually destitute, he was reduced, like Ella, to living in a small rented flat. But he continued to visit the store, where he would treat himself to a coffee in the restaurant – served occasionally by my mother. By then, in his early eighties, he was sadly decrepit, but showed a caring interest in how the waitresses were coping with the devastating German air raids.

He must have been pleased, therefore, when a reporter from the evening paper *The Star* interviewed Mother for an article on how London girls kept working through the Blitz. Ella, photographed looking trim and attractive in her uniform, explained how she lived alone in a Chelsea basement flat. She took the precaution of pinning a notice to her door saying, 'I am here alone, so if anything happens look for me'.

Her little flat was spared but Selfridges was less lucky and its famous Palm Court was reduced to a wilderness of tangled steel and burned timber. Harry Selfridge survived the war to die in 1947. Mother always kept her red-covered staff Store Guide, originally drawn up by the extraordinary retailing genius. At the top of page one it declared: 'Please remember not to use the expression, "Can I help you?" when speaking to a customer.'

Presumably, Ella never asked Mr Selfridge the forbidden question as he sat, shabby and alone, in the restaurant, unrecognised by other customers. They did not know he had built and owned the great emporium – and had coined the phrase 'the customer is always right'.

The first bomb of the war had fallen on the City of London in August 1940. It landed in St Giles' churchyard in the Barbican area and was the precursor of the storm of bombs that was to change the face of the old city. On one night alone, the Germans destroyed eight Wren churches.

Mother took the Blitz in her cheerful stride, but Father was becoming increasingly worried about her safety and looked for a solution. He had been posted to Tangmere RAF station in Sussex as batman to a Wing Commander Thomas Pike and officers were billeted in a nearby country mansion, Northfields, owned by the wealthy Doxford shipping engineering family. On learning that Mrs Doxford was looking to replace a cook, he volunteered Mother for the job. She was taken on and, having inherited some of her mother's skill at cooking, made a great success of the work. I spent the Christmas holiday of 1941 at the house and Mrs Doxford promised to buy me a motorcycle when I was twenty-one if I had refrained from smoking by then. Perhaps she hoped Mother would still be cooking for her. In fact, Mother was soon to move on, breaking our link with the Doxfords.

Back in Broadwell, Alan and I joined the local Boy Scout troop. This was commanded by the church curate Stephen Fowler, who was to remain a friend until his death over forty years later. Also, we had been confirmed by the local bishop in a large church at Coleford. This had been at the commanding 'suggestion' of Mrs Blanch. I have since come to think that young people should be allowed to make their own decision when old enough to understand what they are doing.

We lived well on the farm by wartime standards, our rations augmented by the chickens and their eggs, and there was plentiful milk, cream and homemade butter. Occasionally we had pork – the slaughter of a pig was a particularly bloody ritual in which local lads held down the animal while its throat was cut. Virtually nothing of the carcass was wasted. That, also, applied to the fowls. Mrs Blanch's chicken stew contained everything except the feathers. I would pale as I ate my dishful when a glazed eye glared back balefully from the mess of pottage. The beak and claws were less off-putting – but I shall never forget the day I bit into the gall bladder.

Another hardship was washing in cold water from a rain trough in the yard. In winter, this meant breaking the ice to get at it. But there were lots of good days. During summer holidays Mrs Blanch would take us to local beauty spots such as the famous Symonds Yat. There, we enjoyed the spectacular view of the River Wye far below us, cutting its way through limestone cliffs on its way to Wales. I had never seen any landscape so breathtaking in its beauty before. We picnicked on chicken and stuffing sandwiches as we sat on the Yat rock, looking across at majestic Coppet Hill in the distance. A special treat was an occasional visit to the historic town of Monmouth, birthplace of Henry V, hero of Agincourt, when Mr Blanch attended the sheep and cattle markets in the old square. One summer's day we cycled into the town over the thirteenth-century bridge to watch Alan – a stylish young batsman – play cricket for our school against Monmouth Grammar. Pushing our bicycles uphill on the homeward journey, we stopped for a break and a local lad persuaded me to smoke my first woodbine – but it was not a cigarette from a packet. Wild woodbine hung from the forest trees and boys would break it off when it was dry, light it and puff away. Mrs Doxford would have been disappointed that I had taken this first step. Perhaps it was this forest practice that inspired the Wills tobacco company to name a cigarette after the creeper?

'Aunt' Lil was not a fan of the cinema. But the word spread through the forest communities that it was akin to national duty to see *The Great Dictator*. Made in the USA, the film was a devastating lampoon on Adolf Hitler. It starred and was also written and directed by the world's greatest comedian, Charlie Chaplin. Over breakfast one morning, Lil announced that she would take Alan and me into Coleford to see it. Everyone at church had been talking about it. Indeed, the Rev. Stephen Fowler said it was so funny that no one could take Adolf seriously again.

There was a long queue outside the cinema and we hoped the film would be worth the wait. It was.

Chaplin was born four days before Hitler on 16 April 1889. His superb portrayal of the Führer-like character in the 1940 film transformed him from a much-loved clown into a national hero. Yet in February 2012 it was revealed that just over a decade after this triumph, the American authorities asked Britain's M15 to investigate Chaplin's background. He was suspected of having communist links. Brought up in poverty in South London, he had moved to the USA in 1910 in search of a better life. He sailed back to Britain with his family to attend the premiere of his film *Limelight* in 1952. This was at the height of the Red Scare in the USA. Chaplin denied the accusations and MI5 concluded he was no more than 'a progressive or radical' politically. His move to Switzerland was hardly defecting behind the curtain.

The film inspired me to include a take-off of the Nazi leader in the school's end of term concert. Alan was chosen to play the housepainter-turned-tyrant. With a false moustache and a fringe of hair combed down over his forehead, there was a certain likeness. Not quite a second Chaplin, he did however inspire applause as he barked 'All I want is peace! A piece of Czechoslovakia, a piece of Poland, a piece of France...'

Meanwhile, the war increased in ferocity. From the farmyard one night, we watched a glow in the sky as Bristol burned after a German bombing raid. One day we gave a small cheer in the kitchen as the radio announced that Hitler had invaded the Soviet Union. We were not great strategists but we knew enough about Napoleon's disaster in the Russian wastes to suspect and hope that the German Army had made a serious blunder. Whatever happened, there would be a lot fewer Germans to fight us.

At Tangmere, Wing Commander Thomas Pike had done well commanding No. 219 Squadron. They flew Beaufighters in a night fighter role. A successful pilot himself, he had twice been awarded the DFC and promotion was on the way. Good-looking, with a calm, reflective manner, he never raised his voice to my father who held him in high regard and took a batman's pride in ensuring that his turn-out was impeccable. He was proud, too, when Pike was promoted to Group Captain and given command of the important North Weald Aerodrome, near Epping in Essex. He was to occupy a large country house and Father was told to prepare to move with him. His wife Althea and two young daughters would be moving in, too – and would need a cook.

Bidding farewell to a dismayed Mrs Doxford, Mother was soon on her way to Essex. The Pikes' imposing new home was named Hastings Wood House. set in large grounds with a separate residence for the servants. When they discovered that their house had a guestroom, my parents asked me if I would like to join them. That would mean I could take up my place at Wanstead High School, which had returned from its evacuation in Chippenham. Thanks to the RAF, German bombing raids on London had sharply declined. Although I was happy on the farm I gladly accepted their invitation. Alan had already gone back to London. Soon, so had I, having bade a very fond farewell to 'Uncle' Milson and 'Aunty' Lil. I owed them a lot and promised to keep in touch. I did, even visiting them some ten years later when they had retired from the farm and bought a neat, modern house in nearby Berryhill.

My time in Broadwell had been well spent, but I had made the right choice to leave. My father had also been faced with a choice. An officer senior to Pike named Leigh-Mallory, impressed by his work, had tried to poach him. Unlike Pike, however, he was a brusque, rough-edged character and father found an excuse for not accepting his offer. It was a fortunate decision. Leigh-Mallory, by then Air Chief Marshal, would be killed in an air accident with members of his staff later in the war – and Father, as his batman, would have been aboard that plane. Pike, meanwhile, was heading for more glory and promotion. Just as we were settling into life in the pleasant Essex countryside, he was ordered to take up a new post with Desert Air Force in North Africa. Having the best batman in the RAF, he wanted Father to go with him. What he promised him we never knew, especially as Father was told he would lose his corporal's stripes if he left North Weald, where he had some extra responsibilities. A 'consultation' with my mother became rather heated. Mother gave way and Father headed for the desert. Before he went, however, he had one cause for misgiving. Mrs Pike's sister had been married shortly before to an RAF officer and the wedding reception was held at Hastings Wood House. My father, in charge of the catering arrangements, did his best to make it a culinary success. He chatted up the catering sergeant at North Weald and succeeded in those days of iron rations in supplementing substantially the matrimonial feast. When it was over, Pike thanked him and Mother for producing such a fine spread. Father suggested that the Group

Captain might like to thank the catering sergeant for his help. To Father's dismay there was no thank you for the sergeant. Instead, he received an immediate posting abroad. Pike had no intention of a misuse of rations hindering his climb to the top – which is where he ended up. With a well-earned knighthood, he became Marshal of the Royal Air Force and Chief of Air Staff from 1960-63, and Deputy Supreme Allied Commander Europe, 1964-67.

The treatment of the helpful sergeant made my mother extremely angry. Her temper was not improved by having to find somewhere to live on less money, as Father had given up his stripes. Eventually a flat was found in Leytonstone, a suburb in East London contiguous to Wanstead. Unfortunately, it was in a filthy state and she was in a fury for days as she scrubbed and scoured. I kept out of her way. Father was further out of her way, getting his knees brown in the desert.

I had never heard of Leytonstone, although its neighbour, Leyton, was well known, boasting a professional football team (Orient). It was also dignified by being a parliamentary constituency well represented by Labour's Reg Sorensen MP. I was to learn, however, that Leytonstone's busy, shop-lined High Road had been a major route to Essex and the east coast since Roman times.

The extension eastwards of the railway in Victorian times had given a boost to house building in the area and Leytonstone became the fastest growing town in England in the 1870s and 80s. It might have spread further if it had not been bordered by the protected 6,000 acre Epping Forest and the green open space of Wanstead Flats, dotted with grazing cattle.

Decades after we moved in it was to make news again when it became a dormitory area on the doorstep of the athletes' village built for London's 2012 Olympic Games.

Mother got work in a local cake factory to support us. When

it was my birthday, she nicked some eggs and butter to make me a cake, hiding them under her skirt. As she walked out of the gate the security guard gave her a playful pat on the rear – with disastrous results!

In 1944 the war returned to London with the arrival of Hitler's V-1 flying bomb, the Doodlebug. At school, teachers were stationed on the roof as lookouts and when a V-1 was seen approaching they waited until the engine cut out – the indication it was about to dive to the ground – then sounded a bell if it was near. Ground floor cloakrooms had been reinforced to act as shelters and we would be sent down to them as soon as the warning sirens began to wail. Sometimes the warning would sound in the middle of tests or mock exams, enabling us to swap answers before returning to the classroom. Eventually they came so often that pupils were taught in the shelters, half the school attending in the mornings, and half in the afternoons.

At home, where we occupied the ground floor of an Edwardian purpose-built apartment house, the woman in the flat above had spent a considerable sum on a well-designed brick air raid shelter in the back garden. We all went into it once but did not enjoy the experience. After that, we sought shelter under the stout dining room table or beneath a sturdy wooden dresser that was built into the wall.

One day, cycling home from visiting a friend on the outskirts of Ilford, I heard the dreaded Doodlebug sound and then the ominous cut out of the engine. I started to pedal quickly down a hill until I realised with horror that the flying bomb was pursuing me and that we would meet at the bottom of the slope. Pulling on the brakes, I jumped off the bike and over a low garden wall, flattening myself as the Doodlebug hurtled overhead to its destruction.

When, in June 1944, the Allies landed on the French coast

in the greatest seaborne invasion in history, we hoped the rocket raids would end. Some 18,000 houses were destroyed and 800,000 damaged by the V-1s. By September 1944, however, Home Secretary Herbert Morrison confidently declared that the battle for London had been won. He should have kept his politician's big mouth shut. Next day, the first supersonic missile, the V-2, hit the city. Unlike the V-1, it travelled so fast it gave no warning of its approach. It was a forty-six foot rocket carrying a one-ton warhead. Five hundred fell on London between September 1944 and March 1945. One hit the north west corner of Wanstead High School in December. Luckily, we were all on holiday – a vacation extended while the damage was repaired. About that time, a local air-raid warden asked me if I would be willing to be cycle messenger for his unit and when I said I would, he issued me with a steel helmet and an armband. One day, fooling about in the classroom after lessons, I fell and banged my head on a desk. There was a lot of blood. A teacher dressed the wound. The next day I rode in to school sporting my bloodstained bandage and nonchalantly replied to all concerned enquiries that I had been hurt while on duty as the wardens' messenger during a raid the previous night. In Walter Mitty style, I was determined to have my moment of glory before the war ended.

My father's parents had celebrated their fiftieth wedding anniversary in 1943. With their family dispersed and money short, they did not celebrate with a party. Instead, each of their children received a studio photograph of them, my grandmother looking remarkably robust after rearing her ten-strong brood on slender means in the small terraced house in Faversham. In contrast, my grandfather, worn down by hard physical work, looked rather frail and gentle. In reality he was fit and wiry – and he enjoyed a longer life than my father, who damaged his health by smoking.

One memory I have of my grandfather was when I was taken to see him at work and watched him shovelling coal into a furnace. He was in his sixties and seemed too old for such hard labour. Other, happier, memories have him tending his garden, ablaze with a riot of multi-coloured dahlias or digging his allotment, where prize marrows nestled between beds of potatoes and runs of beans.

Meanwhile, following the defeat of the German Army in North Africa, my father had moved with his air force unit to a new war zone in Italy. Pike had been promoted to Air Commodore – but had failed to get Father a replacement set of corporal's stripes. Now, at last, he was able to see for himself some bits of Europe that Mother had visited with Lina, starting with Naples. Thanks to Mother's descriptions of her travels, I had started to think of making a career out of writing and illustrating travel books after the war. One way or another, either as an author of books or as a newspaper journalist, I wanted to see the world and write about it. I was receiving high marks at school for my essays and artwork and was contributing to the school magazine. Then I broke into the pages of the local newspaper, the *Leytonstone Express and Independent*.

During a blackout, someone I knew had almost cycled into a bomb crater on the nearby common known as Wanstead Flats. I went to inspect the hole. Then I sent off a letter to the editor suggesting that to avoid accidents, German prisoners of war should be put to work filling in the damage made by Nazi bombs and rockets. The letter was well displayed and Mother was surprised when neighbours, assuming she had written it, congratulated her for raising the issue. As for me, I was sure I now had a foot on the road to Fleet Street.

To help the war effort, the school organised a farm camp in the summer holidays at Snap Farm in Wiltshire. Boys were useful in helping to gather in the harvest while manpower was short. Our camp was near the village of Aldbourne and nearby was the base of American paratroopers preparing to drop into the Normandy countryside as part of the great invasion. These young men, members of Easy Company of the 506th Parachute Infantry Regiment, were to become famous for their magnificent exploits in the book and television series *Band of Brothers*. On 6 June 1944, they were dropped behind the Utah beachhead and destroyed German guns that had been creating carnage with a rolling barrage across the sands. Suffering heavy casualties, they were sent back to peaceful Aldbourne after ten days to recover before returning to battle in September. Near the farm camp was a large dump of discarded US Army equipment, mostly clothing, much of it unused. Scavenging through the piles I found a new pair of knee-length leather boots and an unworn waterproof zip-up jacket that I wore for years. Decades later I was reminded of this when I read Max Hastings' account of the battle for Germany 1944-45, entitled *Armageddon*. He wrote; 'Waste was prodigious and contributed mightily to Allied logistical difficulties. Everywhere the armies went, in their wake lay great trails of discarded equipment and supplies.'

As we cycled around the leafy Wiltshire lanes we sometimes met up with companies of young paratroopers on the march. On the corner of one lane a local farmhand pointed out to me a house of advanced design that he said was owned by a Labour politician named Dalton – the famous Hugh with whom I was to become friendly some fourteen years later.

Food was plentiful at the camp but we could not resist trying to catch rabbits to add to the pot. We would chase them as they scurried across the cut cornfields cleared by the combine harvester, and kill them quickly with a sharp blow to the back of the neck. One night I was caught by a teacher, trying to cook one over some candles in our hut. I shall never forget the disgust on his face.

By the winter of 1944 I had established myself as the best cross-country runner in my year and was chosen to run for the school, even though I was a year younger than the other team members. On the sports field, I was running the mile. To help with athletics we were fortunate to have the services of Jim Alford, a renowned Welsh athlete who had won a gold for the mile in the 1938 Empire Games. He arrived at the school early in 1946 after serving as a pilot in the war. Alford, in turn, involved the successful AAA national coach Geoffrey Dyson in training the school's athletics team that, as a result, won virtually every event in the Essex schools' tournaments. Star of the team was Geoffrey Elliott, who went on to represent Britain at the pole vault in the 1948 Olympic Games.

Less enjoyable was the swimming, in the school's ice-cold pool. Some of it was supervised by a sadistic master named Sidney Heaven who, despite his name, did his best to give us hell. He had a long pole with which he would push us under as we struggled in the water. On giving me a sharp prod one day he declared; 'If you were my son, Butler, I'd drown you!'

He nearly did. Sharply sarcastic, he was feared and deeply disliked by pupils at the school but after the war he wisely gave up teaching and apparently did useful administrative work for London education. As reported in *The Times* after his death, there was a large turnout for his memorial service.

As a member of the advanced stream at school, I took the school certificate examination early and matriculated with a distinction in Art and good results in English and History. My plan had been to leave school and apply for a job on a local newspaper, but I was told I was too young to get such a post. Alan Barton and my other friends were all staying on at school to take the Higher School Certificate with a view to trying for a university place or entering a profession such as accountancy or the law. I decided to ask my parents if I could stay on for another year and although Mother could have used some earnings from me, she agreed enthusiastically. I chose subjects to study in the sixth form that would be useful for a travel writer or journalist – English, French, Art and Economics.

When the new term began, I was told I was to be appointed a house captain, the youngest by a year in the school. I was determined my house would be top, and that I would help by winning the school cross-country run. That meant beating a rival house captain, a fine all-round athlete named Geoffrey Pardoe, who was a year older than me. He went on to become one of Britain's leading rocket scientists and directed the Blue Streak rocket test at Woomera, Australia. He was often invited to explain the latest developments to TV audiences. Luckily, I was able to beat him in the cross-country before he got rocket propulsion.

As the war in Europe approached its end, party politics began to re-emerge. The Conservative Party sensed it could cash in on the impending great victory and presumably the popularity of Winston Churchill. Labour politicians, impatient to regain their independence from the wartime coalition, were keen to prepare for a general election. Led by Deputy Prime Minister Clem Attlee, Labour ministers resigned from the government in May 1945, returning to the Opposition frontbench in the Commons. Churchill formed a caretaker government to carry on until polling day. Election fever swept through the country – and through the camps where British servicemen were based abroad.

What with Mother's Labour sympathies, my Conservative-voting father's absence abroad and the outspoken anti-Tory views of Nell's family in Dover, I was bound to give my allegiance to the left. In a mock election at a local youth club, I stood as the Labour candidate and lost to the Liberal. The local newsagent, an active socialist, knowing my talent for painting, asked me to produce two anti-Tory posters for his shop windows. They were duly displayed, one showing an octopus with tentacles spread, representing private monopoly power, coupled with a clarion call for the nationalisation of basic industries. The newsagent told me that the local Labour candidate was very impressed. He was the Rev. Reginald Sorensen, a hard-working Unitarian minister with whom I became friendly.

I went along to neighbouring Woodford to hear the Tory candidate address a public meeting. I had gone with the intention of heckling but the candidate was Winston Churchill and although some of his claims and comments riled me, I was ultimately too in awe of the triumphant old warhorse to challenge him. Despite his historic achievements – sadly marred by some outrageous allegations against his recent Labour colleagues in the coalition government – he was swept from power and Prime Minister Attlee took charge of the country.

With my interest in politics growing, on a visit to Foyles' bookshop in the Charing Cross Road I bought a book by John Strachey entitled *Why You Should Be A Socialist*. It was one of the famous Gollancz Yellow Book series and it became my bible. I was also reading avidly my economics textbooks, especially *Introduction to Economics* by Alec Cairncross, who became Chief Economic Adviser to successive governments in the 1960s. The reading paid off and I gained a distinction in Economics in the Higher School Certificate exam.

Robert Browning was one of the poets whose work I studied for my English Literature exam. I was taken with his conversational style in work like *My Last Duchess*. The savage assassination of the former Italian dictator Benito Mussolini towards the end of the war left a vivid impression on me. He had been recognised while trying to flee across the Swiss border by Italian partisans. He and his mistress were shot. His body was then moved to Milan where it was hung by the feet in the Piazza Loretto, the scene of recent neo-fascist mass executions of hostages. I decided to write a poem about his gruesome end for the school magazine, in the style of Robert Browning:

A Successor Reflects

All these to the Museum Bernardo,
Yes, his sword and his boots and his hat,
Array them on one of the models, but wait –
No, you must not take that –
Not the white coat, his favourite,
All heavy with braid.
He wore that the day of the victory parade.
I can hear the bands still as they played all the way,
See the crowds as they thronged the piazza that day,
See the goose-stepping soldiers who marched in the rear,
They would conquer all Europe in less than a year.
I sat proud at his side along shining white roads
That replaced rutted tracks that had doubled the loads
Of the starved, ill-clad peasants, the beggars, the poor,
Who were reborn in glory and baptised in war.
'I rose with the people,' was what he would say,
But the 'with' changed to 'from' one unfortunate day.
And now they cheer me, that same crowd in the square,
Where he hangs with his jack-booted feet in the air.
Three shots in the back from a patriot's gun.
Ah Bernardo, how soon they forget what is done!
But these thoughts depress me. Take all but the white.
And tell our young hero I'll see him tonight.

The poem appeared in the first post-war edition of the school magazine in the summer of 1946. The editorial noted that it scarcely seemed possible that 'a year ago we were still looking

forward to the long struggle (as we thought) yet lying ahead
– that the atomic bomb, United Nations Organisation, the
Peace Conference, demobilisation were all no more than ideas
in the heads of a few men...'

To help prepare for that final school exam, I had spent a
long weekend of concentrated study at a fine old house in
Thaxted run by the Essex Education Authority. This short
experience of living in with academics so impressed me, that
for the first time, I wondered about the possibility of applying
for a place at university. Although I stayed in Thaxted for only
a few days I fell in love with the little Essex town, with its
timber-framed houses and cobbled lanes. My first view of it
was as I cycled from Wanstead and saw the steeple of the
famous fourteenth-century church soaring above the fields.
Supported by flying buttresses, it rises for 180 feet. Inside, the
church is light and airy thanks to the large, mostly clear, glass
windows. Local merchants, made rich by the wool and cloth
trades, hoped to buy a place in heaven by using their wealth
to enrich the building where gargoyles grimace, gape and grin.
When I first entered the church, the organist was practising
for the Sunday service. I learned that Gustav Holst, when a
local resident, had composed on the fine organ. I heard my
teachers discussing the reputation of the vicar, the Reverend
'Red' Jack Putterill, an active Christian Socialist. From what
they said he seemed a colourful, controversial character and I
was sorry to leave the town without meeting him or hearing
him preach.

While at Thaxted, I also overheard some of the teachers
hotly discussing the implications of the Butler Education Act.
Introduced by the wartime coalition government in January
1944 it was very much the work of Richard Austen 'Rab'
Butler, who had taken over the Board of Education – as the
Education Ministry was then called – in July 1941. Acclaimed

as the first comprehensive measure dealing with education, it had set up a tripartite system of secondary modern schools, technical schools and grammar schools. Introducing the concept of primary education as just the first step in a continuing process, it proposed raising the school leaving age to fifteen without exemption from April 1946.

Butler had entered Parliament as MP for Saffron Walden in 1929, the year of my birth. He had already made himself financially independent by marrying, a few years earlier, Sydney Elizabeth Courtauld, only daughter of Samuel Courtauld, the fabulously wealthy head of the eponymous textile company. As Under-Secretary of State for Foreign Affairs he had defended Chamberlain's policy of appeasement to Hitler, but still Churchill had given him the education post on becoming wartime Prime Minister.

Once the war was over in Europe, Mother and I waited impatiently for my father to be demobilised. He had ended up at Klagenfurt in Austria, where he appeared to be having a good time. At last he knocked at the door and stood there, tanned and fitter than I had ever seen him, surrounded by all his kit and booty, including a six-piece coffee service from Italy. His old job awaited him at the Brown Shipley Bank. One evening, to Mother's distinct disapproval, he took me to the Walthamstow dog track. I won five pounds and the next day put on a 'man of the world' act in the school prefects' hut. On one of my last days at school, as a few of us sprawled there contemplating what the future might hold, I let it be known that I would like to be an *eminence grise*. I had picked up the phrase reading about Cardinal Richelieu. This statement of ambition was received with hoots of derision and a straw boater was lobbed at my head. Thirty years later I was to become involved in providing an *eminence grise* for the new Tory Party leader Margaret Thatcher – my friend and colleague, the extraordinary former communist Sir Alfred Sherman. Perhaps that made me an *eminence grise* at one remove?

It was Mother's ambition that I should learn to play the piano well. Her own mother, Alice, had paid for her to have lessons when she was living in Dover but as Aunt Nell did not own a piano, she had to improvise by drawing piano keys on the white scrubbed kitchen table – an impossible substitute. With Alice's help, she arranged for me to have piano lessons from the age of seven and although I showed no great promise, these continued until I was evacuated. At Gidea Park, I had been much put off the instrument by a sadistic lady teacher who rapped my knuckles and trod sharply on my feet when I was using the pedals. I had no intention of continuing lessons at Broadwell, but there was a piano at the farm and I started at last to play for pleasure.

As soon as Mother and I set up home in Leytonstone and retrieved the family piano from storage, I began to buy sheet music – simple classics and swing – from Woolworths. Some of the jazz pieces I learnt by heart – 'Stardust', 'These Foolish Things', 'Honeysuckle Rose', 'Smoke Gets in Your Eyes' and 'Alligator Crawl'. My party-piece showstopper was 'Honky-Tonk Train Blues' with its shattering opening chords. Composed by Chicago pianist Meade Lux Lewis (born 1905) and recorded in 1936 by Parlophone, it is said to have introduced the 'boogie' style – and the word itself – in to England. There was an active classical music appreciation group at school, but nothing for jazz fans. Using my influence as house captain, I persuaded a young lady teacher to help set one up. Through the resulting club I began to learn more about the pioneers and giants of the jazz age – such as Joe 'King' Oliver of New Orleans, one of the first exponents of twentieth-century jazz trumpeting. After moving to Chicago, he formed his own band and by 1922 had been joined by his protégé, the young Louis Armstrong, who, unsurpassed as a trumpet player and possessing an infectious joy of life, was to further the development of jazz like no other.

I went to the cinema on Saturday mornings to watch adventure films featuring such schoolboys' heroes as Jungle Jim, Flash Gordon, Hopalong Cassidy and Buck Rogers. These rowdy sessions were known as the 'threepenny rush' and there was a ruthless scramble to get the front seats in the balcony – not for a better view of the screen but so we could throw nutshells, apple cores and other assorted small missiles at the heads of those in the stalls.

In the mid-1940s, another Saturday morning treat for me was to see Ted Heath's band play at the Paris Cinema near Piccadilly Circus. Trombonist Heath formed his band in 1945 aiming to compete with the Americans. His lead trumpeter was the brilliant Kenny Baker and on drums was the energy-packed Jack Parnell. On the more 'pure' jazz front I went at weekends to the crowded, beer-soaked Cooks Ferry Inn at Edmonton, north London, to hear trumpeter Freddy Randall lead his rumbustious Chicago-style band. There, too, I first heard the exuberant trumpet playing of Humphrey Lyttleton, whose aristocratic background and wartime service as a Guards officer gave him added glamour. Inspired by the playing of Louis Armstrong, Humph bought his first trumpet at the age of fifteen while at Eton.

Aged seventeen, I knew that I would soon have to do my national service. I was keen to go abroad but with the war in Europe over, I could not be sure of an overseas posting with the army. I saw a recruiting advertisement in a national newspaper for the Palestine police. It showed a smart armed member of the force standing in old Jerusalem and I sent off for the necessary papers. Then it was announced that an Indian Army recruiting officer was to visit the school and I decided it was a better prospect. I had seen the film *Lives of a Bengal Lancer* and pictured myself in turban and fine uniform doing a spot of pig-sticking before an admiring crowd. I filled in the application form and after two days of tests in a hotel in Marylebone, I was informed that I had been accepted as an Indian Army officer cadet and should report to the Guards Depot at Caterham in September.

The depot was the bleak training centre for new recruits to the Brigade of Guards. Built in 1875, it was known as 'the Drill Factory' and its reputation for strict discipline was legendary. Years later my occasional drinking companion Auberon Waugh, who served there in 1957, described it as; 'a complete hell-hole staffed by sadistic morons – a place where no glimmer of kindness was allowed to show through.' Austere, outdated barrack blocks stared down on barrack squares, some of which were roofed so that drill could continue in all weathers. 'Thank goodness I'll only be here for six weeks! Then India ... here I come!' I thought. But that was not to be.

On our first morning, we were paraded to await our Commanding Officer. He was rather overweight with a florid complexion and a large posterior. Major 'Bum' Nicholls, of the Indian Army's Frontier Force, looked a trifle embarrassed. In fruity, apologetic tones he revealed that the government had decided that, in view of current moves towards independence, no more British personnel would be sent there for commissioning in the Indian Army. We were the last intake of Indian Army Officer Cadets and, instead of being sent to Bangalore after completing our six weeks basic training at Caterham, we would have to pass a War Office Selection Board to be accepted for training for Commissions in the British Army. As there were hundreds of us, that process would take some time.

Anger welled up inside me. I had been enticed to volunteer at seventeen for the army under what now seemed to be a false prospectus. Surely the politicians and military chiefs foresaw the situation in time to cancel our engagement and give us the opportunity to think again? Or were they really so short-sighted and incompetent?

At Wanstead High, our enthusiastic, inspiring English Literature teacher Miss Ida Jacobs had introduced me to the novels of E.M. Forster. In preparation for my enrolment in the Indian Army, I had read *A Passage to India*. As events had transpired, it was now for me a case of *No Passage to India* – Forster's exotic India of the Raj was almost a country of the past.

4

Great Brittain

The problem of self-government for India was one of the most urgent to face the new Labour Government after the war. Key members of the Cabinet had sympathy with the Indian political parties' aspiration to achieve independence, but a major obstacle was that of the deep and bitter antagonism between the Hindu and Muslim populations. A Cabinet mission went to India in the spring of 1946 to try to resolve the problem and, working with the Viceroy Lord Wavell, made some progress with the opposing sects. They created the Viceroy's Council that included the Hindu leader, Pandit Nehru. Nehru and his Congress Party favoured an Indian state covering the whole of the peninsular but Mr Jinnah, leader of the Muslim League, was determined to see a separate Muslim state established. As talks became bogged down, communal trouble spread.

In the month before I arrived at Caterham, Calcutta exploded in what was described as 'berserk fury'. Some 4,000 were killed and 10,000 injured. Atrocious crimes were committed. On one night alone, 450 corpses were cleared from the city streets by 3 battalions of British – as distinct from Indian Army – troops. The military were having a grim time. The immediate cause of the bloodletting was the decision of Mr Jinnah to have a Muslim day of 'direct action' on 16 August in protest at what he alleged to be unfair treatment of Muslims by the interim government.

Speeches by leading men of both the Congress Party and the Muslim League became more and more inflammatory. A British official described India as being like a great liner at sea, holed and on fire, with a cargo of high explosives.

As the politicians argued and the government dithered, within the army the famous Gurkha regiments were becoming restless. In the absence of any clear policy about the future, suspicion grew that they would be handed over to India. Men started to take their discharge, as increasing numbers of British soldiers stationed in India were being demobilised.

That was the scene as I arrived at Caterham as an Indian Army Officer Cadet on that warm September day. The following morning, as I walked away from the parade ground, I should have been relieved, not aggrieved, that I so narrowly avoided being sent into the impending disaster. I did realise that for many of my new comrades the disappointment was far greater than mine as they belonged to families with a long and proud tradition of service in the Indian Army – an army famous for its discipline, regimental loyalty and *esprit de corps*. In the recent war, it had played an important role in Britain's campaigns in North Africa, Italy and Burma. For some of the cadets, a chain stretching back a hundred years had been broken.

As my anger subsided I decided not to simply accept the situation – I would change course. During the next two years I would take every opportunity to study with the aim of winning a place at university. Friends I had left at school were studying for their inter-BSc (Economics). I already had my distinction in Economics and now set about finding if I could take the remaining BSc subjects while completing national service. Those subjects were Economic History, Economic Geography, British Constitution and Logic. I discovered that anyone seeking to study in the army could call on a lot of assistance from its Education Corps.

Immediately, however, I had to cope with daily life in the Drill Factory. On arriving at Caterham, we had been formed alphabetically into platoons by senior cadets of a previous intake. My platoon therefore contained cadets whose surnames began with A, B or C. Virtually all were from public schools. One was Michael Auden, related to the poet W.H. Auden, whose work and early participation in the Spanish Civil War I much admired. Another was Derek Barton-Chapple, the son of Wing Commander Harry Barton-Chapple who had worked closely with John Logie Baird in developing television. Derek's brother Richard was a highly-successful writer of comedy for TV in the 1960s-70s. He changed his name to Waring thinking 'Barton-Chapple' too cumbersome for the entertainment business – and Derek, in due course, followed suit. Tall and handsome, with a polished manner, Derek took up an acting career. He eventually married the actress Dorothy Tutin, who was made a Dame of the British Empire in 2000. I first saw her when in 1954 she played Sally Bowles in the dramatisation of Christopher Isherwood's *I am a Camera*. Derek bunked next to me. He was only a year older but I was impressed by his cultured manner and confident style. He was a talented mimic and entertained us with his impersonations of the NCOs and officers who plagued our lives.

It was due to Derek that I first learned about *netsuke*. These traditional, Japanese, hand-carved toggle closures for garments had evolved over several centuries into a uniquely special form of intricate miniature sculpture much sought after by collectors. Derek, aged nineteen, was such a collector. Sometimes, on a day off, I would go with him in search of items for his collection – perhaps a crouching mouse or a hare. I was reminded of Derek and our expeditions when Edmund de Waal's novel, *The Hare with Amber Eyes*, relating the history of a family's valuable collection of *netsuke* over two centuries, received much publicity in recent times.

Our first full day at Caterham was spent being kitted out and shorn. Although we wore Indian Army flashes, our cap badge, backed by a circular white disc, was the Braganza lamb and flag of the Queen's Royal Regiment – the Second of Foot, or, as they were jokingly known, the 'Mutton Lancers'. If we failed the course we would be 'returned to unit', to the regimental depot of the Queen's. Our officers were of various Indian Army regiments. A Major Thistleton Dyer of the Baluch Regiment introduced himself as our platoon commander.

Back in our barrack room, we were shown how to lay out our kit for inspection and carry out daily chores. The floor had to be polished using a bumper – a pad fixed to a long handle – until it shone like glass. Our beds, consisting of three planks supported by low trestles and covered with three thin 'biscuits' in a row to form a mattress, had to be spotless. Our three blankets (no sheets) were wrapped around the biscuits, squared off with the aid of cardboard, to be piled neatly at the head of the bed for inspection purposes. Equipment, such as fire buckets, had to be burnished. Some items were whitened with Blanco. Brigade of Guards battle honours painted on the walls shone from a regular application of oil administered by Guards recruits.

We were also spared the unpleasant task of cleaning the latrines that stood in a line at one end of the square outside our barrack block. That treat was reserved for hapless Guardsmen who had been put on a charge for some (usually petty) breach of discipline. One day a young Guardsman was found hanging from a beam in one of the latrines. Caterham had broken him.

Outside our barrack room were the pathetically inadequate washing facilities, consisting of scarred and worn basins sunk into black slate surrounds – three for every twenty men. To add to the struggle of trying to shave and keep clean, these basins were also used to Blanco our web equipment and were often in a mucky state when the first cadets arrived for their ablutions in the morning. Cleaning equipment took up much of our time in the evenings. Web belts and anklets had to be blancoed; brass fittings, buttons and badges made brilliant; boots, issued to us with a dull patina, had to shine; toe caps boned with implements such as toothbrush handles until they looked like black glass. I didn't have the knack with toecaps so I offered to blanco for a friend if he would 'bull my boots'.

We were inspected minutely every day. On Friday mornings there was the platoon commander's kit inspection with all items of equipment laid out in regulation pattern on our beds. Failure to pass the inspection could mean loss of a weekend pass out of the camp. But for the first four weeks no one was allowed out of camp anyway, unless on a route march.

To someone like me, who had enjoyed the comforts and freedom of home life, all this was pretty hard to take. But the ex-public schoolboys – who made up about eighty per cent of our intake – took it cheerfully in their stride. It was not a lot worse than being back at school and the food was better and more plentiful. Drill, at first without rifles then with arms, took up much of our time. Although we were surrounded by Guardsmen, only one of our drill sergeants came from the brigade. Appropriately, his name was Guard. He was a sergeant in the Grenadiers who taught us drill at the Guards' pace. He was steady, patient and entirely unflappable. He never screamed and he got the best out of us. We held him in high regard – unlike some of the county regiment drill sergeants at the depot whom we grew to despise for their tantrums and bullying, sadistic methods. I began to understand how sergeants were occasionally shot in the back 'by accident' by their own men on going into action.

We were continually checked for personal turnout, and, in view of the inadequate facilities for cleaning equipment and pressing clothes, this was a nagging worry. When we were allowed home for weekend leave, however, my ex-batman father would get to work on my battle dress and great coat with his iron. I would return to camp to be congratulated at Monday morning muster parade for my smartness. I was also winning approval for my cross-country running and was chosen to run for the company – an accomplishment that gave me the privilege of leaving the camp on my own for practice runs. These would take me to a nearby tearoom where I would relax with a bun and a drink. Then, when some of the senior cadets from a previous intake left, I won a place in the company rugby team, which took us on match outings to Sandhurst and Windsor. Things were looking up.

Come November I was given overnight leave to attend Wanstead High School's annual prize giving. To my parents' delighted pride I was called to the platform four times – to receive the local authority's Charter Cup essay prize from the Mayor; the Cockhouse captain's efficiency prize; my Higher School Certificate and a newly-awarded prize for Economics. My parents had sacrificed so much to enable me to stay at school that I was relieved to show them I had not wasted my time. Travelling home on the bus to Leytonstone, Mother encouraged me to think about university. 'We'll support you,' she said. 'Don't worry about the money.'

But I did.

I decided I would need a good grant and, to save money, would need to live at home. That meant aiming for London University and, within it, the famous London School of Economics. No one in my family had ever been to university – only about two per cent of the population enjoyed that distinction. I had already signed up for a London University extra-mural course in the subjects needed to complete my inter-BSc (Economics). Remembering my Kipling, I was determined to fill every minute 'with sixty seconds worth of distance run.'

Then, to add to our discomfort at Caterham, came the severe winter of January/February 1947 – the worst in living memory. The country was covered by a thick blanket of snow and whipped by Arctic winds. Fuel became a priority in the freezing conditions, but the coal dumps were frozen solid. The road and rail transport needed to shift supplies was brought to a virtual standstill.

The previous summer in Dover we had rejoiced with Aunt Nell and her family that the government's bill to nationalise the coal industry had passed through Parliament. On 1 January 1947, vesting day – the day the new act would come into force – the National Coal Board flag had been flown for the first time above the collieries. But overshadowing the celebrations was the spectre of an imminent coal shortage.

The output of deep-mined coal had slumped dramatically since 1939 from 231 million tons to 182 million tons a year. In January 1946, Prime Minister Attlee had warned that lack of coal exports was seriously afflicting our overseas trade but his Fuel Minister, Emmanuel ('Manny') Shinwell, appeared not to take the situation seriously, announcing publicly that there would be no fuel crisis. However, as his deputy Hugh Gaitskell was to point out, Shinwell had no concept of organisation or planning. Like Mr Micawber, he took the view that there was no need to take unpopular decisions as something would turn up.

As we froze in our barracks, we heartily wished that something would turn up. With no fuel for our barrack room stoves we were forced to make briquets with coal dust and cement. We spent hours sweeping snow from the barrack squares so that drill could continue, but that was one way of keeping warm. Outside the camp, factories were closing for want of fuel and for long spells people had no electricity in their homes. The government was castigated for incompetence. Ashamed, I kept quiet about my Labour leanings when my fellow cadets, mostly Tory by upbringing, grumbled angrily about the situation and expressed the hope that the Conservatives would soon be back in power. Michael Foot, with whom I was to become friendly some twenty years later, was to write of the fuel crisis; 'The shock left its wounds and tremors everywhere – on the economy, in the Cabinet, throughout the country and the Labour Movement. Never did the Labour Government recover its first dashing confidence.'

It was on the edge of Caterham's parade ground that I began one of the most important friendships of my life. I was on my way to the Church Army canteen when I saw a figure I recognised. I had last seen it a few years before, wearing a boater and wheeling a bicycle towards the prefects' hut at Wanstead High School. It was Alan Root, then school captain and held in awe for achieving a distinction in every subject he had taken at School Certificate and then Higher School Certificate. Now he stood before me in the uniform of a Grenadier Guard sergeant – and I noticed that he was wearing shoes, not boots.

As I was several years younger than Alan, he had not known me at school. I quickened my pace, as one did when approaching a senior NCO, and marching up to him said; 'Excuse me, Sergeant, were you at Wanstead High School?'

Being Alan, when the call-up for war service came he decided to join one of the best infantry regiments. He had not realised, however, that to become an officer in the Guards one required not so much super intelligence as family connections. The regiment soon realised, however, that they had a recruit of exceptional brainpower. Alan could learn foreign languages at high speed so they sent him on a special one-year course in German at Oxford University. This was to prepare him for being dropped behind enemy lines, only the enemy collapsed before he could be deployed against them. He was then sent on a Russian language course so he could liaise with our Red Army allies. When the war in Europe ended it was decided to train him in Japanese as the conflict continued in the Far East. To Alan's relief, VJ Day was celebrated before he was fluent.

When I met him at Caterham, Alan was waiting for a War Office Selection Board with the intention of being commissioned in the Intelligence Corps. Within a year he had been promoted to captain and was using his Russian skills to do important work in Berlin. He then read Economics at Cambridge where he gained a Double First before going on to Stanford University Business School in California for his postgraduate degree. From there, I imagined he would return to a top job in London and looked forward to renewing our ties. But to both our amazement, no company in England was interested in his qualifications. A top US company soon recruited him and he returned there to be highly successful. His experience throws some light on the way the old boy network still controlled much of British industry and commerce in the early 1950s, stifling initiative and progress.

We would see Alan when he returned to the UK for holidays and my wife and I visited him in Las Vegas, celebrating our fortieth wedding anniversary in a nightclub in that sybaritic city, light years from the ascetic strictures of Caterham.

Alan's mother and I also got on well, from our first meeting at their home in Bishops Stortford in 1949. As a schoolgirl she won a scholarship to James Allen's Girls' in Dulwich, where Gustav Holst taught her music. In due course my daughter Caroline attended the same school and accompanied Mrs Root to a reunion where she was the second oldest 'old girl' on parade.

We were now well into 1947 and I was beginning to wonder if my turn with a War Office Selection Board would ever come. Despite all the sports, the endless repetition of drill and inspections was beginning to pall. I was, however, now well into my university correspondence course and was getting time to study for my first exam. Major Thistleton Dyer had moved on and our new platoon commander, a Captain Bailey of the Gurkhas, was helpful and understanding. He, too, had to pass a selection board to further his ambition – to gain a Commission in the Royal Marines. When we found out he had failed we were all surprised and saddened. Then, at last, I was told to report for a War Office Selection Board in early April at a unit near Haywards Heath. Up to then the WOSB had run until early afternoon on a Friday and the results awaited our CO on the Monday morning. It had therefore become a tradition for cadets to take a forty-eight-hour weekend away from camp in the knowledge that no one would be asking for them until muster parade on Monday.

For some reason our WOSB tests ended mid-morning on the Friday, but not realising the routine had been changed, I left Haywards Heath for a long weekend at home. On returning to camp on Sunday evening I was confronted by a stern Under Officer who wanted to know why I had not returned to Caterham on Friday afternoon. For the first time ever, the WOSB results had reached the CO before Monday. I was in serious trouble. I was marched into Captain Bailey's office on a charge before even knowing if I had passed the selection board. If I had, would he now ask for the result to be rescinded? Had I spent all those months in the hell-hole of Caterham only to be robbed of my chance to get a commission in the British Army?

Bailey looked stern and sentenced me to two weeks confined to barracks. Then, almost as an afterthought, he said I had passed the WOSB and that if I was to get a commission I had better improve my conduct smartly. As I was marched off at the double I felt my legs shaking. It had been a close-run thing.

My friend Derek Barton-Chapple had discussed with me what arm of the service we should try to join. With infantry regiments overloaded with officers following the war, one needed strong family connections to have any hope of being accepted. We therefore decided to apply for the corps with the shortest training period at the Officer Cadet Training Unit (OCTU). That turned out to be the Royal Army Ordnance Corps. We had little idea what it did – but having been chased around the barrack squares at Caterham for eight months, that we would have to endure only eight weeks of further training before winning our 'pip' sold it to us. I was ordered to attend at Mons Barracks, Aldershot, at a date in early May.

My first reaction on arriving was one of pleasant relief. Our barrack room was well equipped, we had sheets on the beds and the washing facilities were perfectly adequate. What a contrast to squalid Caterham. As I exchanged my Indian Army shoulder flashes for those of the Queen's Royal Regiment I shelved my regret at not making it to India. The incompetence of the Attlee government in handling my call-up was typical of the disgraceful manner in which the handover to the Indian and Muslim leaders was to be rushed through without proper planning. Despite warnings of growing violence, the chiefs of staff were ordered not to reinforce our badly-stretched troops in India. So many soldiers had been transferred out that, eventually, for every soldier left behind there were some 40,000 Indians to control.

Lord Wavell, Viceroy of India, warned Attlee of the urgent need for decisions regarding the future borders of Pakistan, the proposed new Muslim state. To prepare for Britain's impending scuttle, Attlee replaced weary but experienced Wavell with ambitious, pushy Earl Mountbatten. A British barrister was given a mere six weeks to recommend the new borderline between India and Pakistan. Perhaps hardened by the death toll he had witnessed on the Western Front in the First World War, Attlee displayed little horror at the slaughter in India that followed his government's handover of power.

After my initial good impression of Mons, less welcome was what took place the following morning at the muster parade for the new intake. As we stood on the great square, rank by rank, we were suddenly conscious of a hush amongst the NCOs. A large figure in the uniform of a Regimental Sergeant Major of the Coldstream Guards now loomed over us. It was RSM Ronald Brittain, all six feet three inches and twenty-one stone of him. His Sam Brown belt and size thirteen boots gleamed in the early morning sunlight. At any moment we were about to hear for the first time what was reputed to be the loudest voice in the army – a voice that, on a good day, could control a squad of men half a mile away.

After standing us at ease, he informed us that we would call him 'Sir' and he would address us in the same way. 'The difference being,' roared 'The Voice', 'you will mean it!'

He then announced to the parade that present were some gentlemen cadets who had enjoyed the great privilege of learning their drill and discipline at the Guards Depot. He ordered the Queen's Royal Regiment Cadets to fall out and reform as a squad at the front of the parade. As our hearts sank to our polished boots, he announced that we were to be his demonstration drill squad and wasted no time in putting us through our paces. 'Oh God,' I thought. 'Will this drill hell never end?'

Over the next few weeks we got to know all of his famous parade ground expressions. As we marched around his high-pitched voice would suddenly intrude; 'Get hold of yourself Sir! You're idle Sir! You're like a pregnant duck Sir!'

His beady eye missed nothing. As we stood on parade his voice would suddenly rise to the high-pitch of controlled indignation. Directing it to the NCO in charge he would shout; 'SERGEANT! That cadet in the Queen's! Number three platoon, number four file, centre rank. He's idle, bone-idle! Take his name!'

And in a final explosion of exasperation he would declaim; 'I've never seen the like of it in all my life!'

The most terrifying experience would be to have him personally inspect you. A mere smear on your footwear and he would have you booked for 'idle boots!' A spec of Blanco on your hand was enough to have you booked for 'dirty flesh on parade!' And if he stood behind your back you might hear him demand in a querulous bellow; 'Am I hurting you Sir? I ought to be Sir! I'm standing on your hair! Get it cut – today!'

One story told of him concerned a soldier he saw freewheeling on a bicycle near the parade ground. Suddenly the cyclist was brought to a wobbling halt by the RSM's roar; 'You there soldier! You're idle pedalling! Get a move on!'

Towards the end of my eight weeks at Mons, I was chosen for picket duty one evening and as we stood awaiting orders Brittain came marching by. I tensed as he swerved towards us and began to inspect our turnout. I was fairly confident I was up to standard. But I was wrong. In the hot summer weather I had produced a sweat stain on the band of my beret. I could feel his eyes boring into my beret. 'You've got an idle cap band Sir! An idle cap band! Take his name Sergeant!'

Luckily that was the only time at Mons I was put on a charge. If it happened too often a cadet was 'returned to unit', his commission hopes dashed. At Okehampton battle camp I had another near squeak when I dropped the platoon mortar in a bog. With the help of a mate I retrieved and cleaned it before an NCO or officer could discover my blunder.

So came the day of the passing-out parade, with proud parents invited to attend the spectacle. I had missed winning the cross-country trophy by some fifty yards – and there was nothing for the runner-up. All I had to do now was to carry out the same old drill for another hour and then march off to don my officer's uniform with its one shiny pip on the shoulder. But as time ticked on I began to feel increasingly faint in the heat of the morning and an awful fear gripped me; I was going to pass out literally on the passing out parade. Then a voice whispered quietly from behind me as a strong hand gripped the back of my web belt and held me upright; 'Stand firm cadet – you're nearly there.'

It was our platoon sergeant. Luckily, because I was standing in the middle of the back row, he had been able to come to my rescue without anyone noticing the incident. I left Mons and RSM Brittain, who by the time he retired in 1954 had drilled over 40,000 officer cadets and who, for all his devotion to spit and polish, had gained a well-earned reputation for fairness and decency.

Following a short leave, which provided an opportunity for swaggering around London in my new uniform, I reported to an RAOC unit at Tidworth to be taught just what the Ordnance Corps was all about. Derek Barton-Chapple joined me there. For much of the time I sat with eyes glazed in the lecture room as the accounting procedure for army stores – involving multitudes of various coloured forms – was spelt out. The prospect of getting involved in all that bumf for my second year of national service depressed me. Luckily, however, as I did not shine in the final test papers, some realistic officer responsible for allocating us to units wisely posted me to the Corp's Regimental Depot, in Feltham, Middlesex. There it would be my task to smarten up drafts ready for embarkation overseas. The scene was set for more drill and bull but this time I would be giving the orders. It was an agreeable posting with a mess full of interesting characters, many of them ex-infantry men waiting to be reallocated or demobilised. One was a major from the Burma Rifles. Another, a captain from the Indian Army who told how he had been on an operation to overthrow the troublesome 'King of Sind'. When they entered his palace they found there a large, heavy safe. Deciding not to risk blowing open the door in case it was full of fragile treasures, they took it, with much sweat and effort, back to HQ. An expert locksmith was found and eventually the door swung open. It was full of pornographic pictures.

There can be no doubt that the worst chore in any unit is that of messing officer. As I was the most junior officer at the depot, it was given to me. I bought a book on basic cooking, food presentation and dining room etiquette. Despite its help there never seemed to be enough of the right ingredients for the endless curry dishes demanded by the more senior officers who had served in and around India. Faced with the agony of mess dining-in nights, when all the officers would dress in their best and the colonel would sit at the head of the table, I would fortify myself with a few strong gins. One night, when as junior officer I had to propose the loyal toast of 'Gentleman! The King!', the drink got the better of me. I rose a little unsteadily and raising my glass, said; 'Kentlemen! The Gin!'

There was a momentary horrified silence, then, pretending they had not heard, the assembled officers got the toast back on course. The colonel cornered me later and told me to attend his office in the morning. As he was a rugby football fan and I had been chosen to play for the Corps, he pulled his punches. He even expressed the view that being messing officer when so young in a mess such as ours could be a stressful and difficult job. Yet he left me in it and so, despite the fact I was enjoying my rugby, I decided to apply for an overseas posting. I had another six months to serve and had been accepted by the London School of Economics for the university year beginning in September.

Another unpopular job fobbed off on to junior officers was that of defending soldiers in trouble at courts martial. Despite the fact I was aged eighteen and obviously inexperienced, I appeared as defending officer at a string of such courts held near Sloane Square, Chelsea. The charge was usually Absent Without Leave (AWOL) and the defendant's excuse invariably involved a pregnant girlfriend or a young wife unable to cope with a domestic problem. As the Regimental Depot handled drafts for overseas postings, most of those going AWOL were men trying to avoid being sent abroad. I cannot recall getting anyone acquitted, but I produced some heart-rending pleas in mitigation. Apparently, I had been overdoing the histrionics. One day, when we paused for lunch, the senior officer of the court said to a captain from my unit involved in another case; 'Advise young Butler to ease up on the sob stuff or he'll have us all in bloody tears!'

As messing officer I had learned a lot about the problems of catering on rations. I was therefore full of sympathy for the officials who had to produce the wedding breakfast for 150 following the marriage ceremony of Princess Elizabeth and Prince Philip in November 1947. It was made known that it would be an 'austerity' affair. The Princess had been given 200 extra clothing coupons by the government as a contribution to her trousseau. I listened to the wedding ceremony on a radio in the groundsman's hut at the depot, where I had gone to collect a rugby ball before my first match in the corps team.

It was while I was playing rugby for the Ordnance Corps that I had the unforgettable experience of meeting a famous Corps character – the bristling Brigadier Terence Clarke. 'Meeting' is perhaps not the word. The former heavyweight army boxer, six feet three inches tall and weighing in at twenty stone, landed on my back in a rough-and-tumble game in the officers' mess after the match. He was a fearsome figure as he looked down at my crumpled form, with his hairy cheeks and huge fists. He revived me with a large brandy. Many years later I reminded him of our introduction when he was Tory MP for Portsmouth and I was a lobby correspondent at the House of Commons. He placed a great hand on my shoulder and marched me off to the nearest bar for another brandy.

A regular officer before the Second World War, he was involved in the disastrous Norway expedition in 1940. He has been remembered, as a senior ordnance officer, uttering mighty oaths to the Nordic gods as he cursed those who had dispatched the wrong stores in boxes carrying no identification lying safely back in their beds in Britain. It was not an episode of which the Ordnance Corps was proud.

By the end of March I was in charge of a draft heading for the British Army of the Rhine, via Harwich and the Hook of Holland. I gave a sigh of relief. No more messing officer worries, playing alchemist with meagre rations. When we disembarked I was surprised to discover how much more food – including delicious white bread – the Dutch had to eat than those I had left behind in post-war Britain. The previous July, the Attlee Government had even been forced to introduce bread rationing for two years – which had not happened even during the war.

The member of the government who had the unpopular task of bringing in the scheme was the Minister for Food John Strachey, whose book on basic socialism had been my political bible. Much to the annoyance of more senior ministers, such as Hugh Dalton, he had wobbled and wavered over its introduction. He was a favourite target for the rowdy Tory 'yah boo' brigade in the Commons.

After a brief stop at RAOC headquarters in Germany I set off to join my new unit – a vehicle company based on a former Luftwaffe aerodrome on the outskirts of Oldenburg, a charming little town in the northwest providing easy access to the coast and the Friesian Islands. Despite its traditional appearance Oldenburg was famous for the fact that, as German morale began to disintegrate towards the end of the First World War, some of its citizens created a Communist republic there, with an ex-navy stoker as president.

The Friesian island of Norderney was famous for its naturist beaches and I would go there at the weekends for a meagre German supper and a night at the dance hall. The next morning I would rendezvous on the more demure stretch of the beach with the teenage girls I had quickstepped with the night before.

The townspeople of Oldenburg were fond of light opera – especially *The Merry Widow* and *White Horse Inn* by Franz Lehar. Attending productions in the town's little opera house, I was delighted by the lusty way in which the audience joined in the choruses. I also saw *Peter Grimes* by Benjamin Britten being toured by a British company intent on spreading modern British culture. It was only Britten's second opera, composed a few years before, and it would establish him as an important composer. I suspect the people of Oldenburg preferred Lehar. I did.

Above: Alice Bond (Mrs Waller), the author's grandmother, in her early forties.

Left: 'Lina' – Caroline Offley Shore (née Sinnickson), 1908.

Top left: Ella Bond, the author's mother, aged seven, sitting on the moon.

Top right: Ella in her early twenties.

Bottom right: Frederick Butler, the author's father, serving with the Desert Air Force, at Klagenfurt, Austria, 1945.

Bottom left: Ella and Fred on their wedding day, August 1928.

Top: Fred with the author in Wanstead High School uniform, 1942.
Bottom left: 'Angel Face' – the author as a choir boy at St. Saviour's Church, Chelsea, 1937.
Bottom right: Evelyn Butler (née Luetchford), the author's wife.

The author, aged 18, in the uniform of a newly commissioned Ordnance Corps 2nd Lieut. 1947.

5

Man of the World

For the first time in my life I was in a foreign country, and it was exciting. With only six months to serve before my demobilisation I intended to see as much of Germany as possible.

Internationally, however, tension was growing. A month before my move to the British Army of the Rhine, the Cold War between the Soviet and Western blocs had turned yet chillier. Russian-backed Communists seized power in Czechoslovakia and the West European states responded with a fifty-year defence pact against armed attack in Europe signed by Britain, France, Belgium, The Netherlands and Luxembourg.

In British-occupied Western Germany, not far from the Russian zone, I was now in the front line. I knew that if the Soviet leaders were rash enough to launch their forces at the West they would sweep over us before the threat of nuclear retaliation brought them to a halt. Still, no one in the Officers' Mess at Oldenburg seemed too worried by the situation. Many of the officers had German girlfriends. One had married into the Steinhager gin family. There was no shortage of that beverage in the mess. Over-consumption could bring on the 'Steinhager twitch'. 'Have a good time!' appeared to be the order of the day.

When I reported to the Commanding Officer he was impressed

that I was due to join the London School of Economics in September. Assuming that an economist would be an expert on time-and-motion study, he asked me to give some thought to improving procedures for receiving, storing and issuing vehicles and spare parts. Meanwhile, he put me in charge of the motorcycle park that seemed to stretch for acres. I recalled Mrs Doxford's promise to present me with a motorcycle if I did not smoke before I was twenty-one. At nineteen, I now had many hundreds at my disposal but never got round to riding one. Instead, I took a short driving course and from then on relied on a jeep to get me around the former aerodrome. The staff sergeant who passed me fit to drive decided to register that I was also able to drive a great range of vehicles that I had never even sat in, including the huge tank transporter. However, officers were not allowed to drive outside the camp area, so I was allocated a cheerful young German driver named Hans, whose motto was also 'Have a good time'!

As at Feltham, there were a number of ex-Indian Army officers in the unit. As my interview with the CO ended on my first morning he said; 'Ah, it's Tuesday. Curry night in the mess. See you there at seven o'clock.'

I forced a smile, thinking; 'Oh God, bloody curry, but at least it's not up to me to produce it!'

And I recalled how when the mess cat had disappeared at Feltham some wag swore it ended up as kitty korma.

Security at night on the former German air force aerodrome that housed the vehicle company was in the hands of a band of tough-looking, trigger-happy Yugoslavs who had been forced to flee their troubled country at the end of the war. Their problem was that they had belonged to the ruthless right-wing army that had spent as much time fighting Tito's equally ruthless communist partisans as the unhappy German army of occupation. When Tito took control, they took to their heels.

A popular pastime at night was to drive with these cut-throats around the aerodrome in jeeps equipped with searchlights to shoot rabbits for the mess cooking pot with their guards' rifles. This sport made it dangerous at times for anyone returning late to camp, as bullets whistled through the trees.

An ex-Indian Army Officer enrolled me in the unit's hockey team. But my big athletic breakthrough came on the unit's sports day when I won the mile by a comfortable margin and was in the winning relay team. Prizes were presented by Colonel Bill Dansie, the dapper officer in charge of all ordnance vehicle depots in BAOR. He warmly congratulated me and suggested to my CO that I was just the young officer needed to supervise the training of the Royal Army Ordinance Corps team for the coming BAOR sports meeting. Members of the team were told to report to Hamburg for ten days where a German athletics coach would put us through our paces. Unfortunately, the nightlife in the naughty city undid all the good work put in on the sports ground and the members of the team were not in great physical shape by the time they returned to their units. At the big BAOR sports day we did not perform well and I subsequently kept out of Colonel Dansie's way.

My favourite haunt in Hamburg was the magnificent Four Seasons Hotel. It provided me with luxury I had never before encountered. Returning from there to my unit one night I suddenly realised that Hans had lost his way. There was no street lighting and we were bumping and crunching over rubble and broken glass. Ahead of us we could see in the headlamps gaunt skeletal remains of buildings looming over small hills of bricks. Suddenly figures flitted across the road, disappearing into cellars where they were living like rats. We had strayed into the remains of the night of horror when British bombers destroyed much of the industrial area of the city. Blocks of workers' flats were engulfed in the legendary firestorm. Even the normally cheerful Hans was silent as he reversed the car at speed to find our proper route.

The destruction of the city port by Allied bombers had come in late July 1943, following a leaflet raid warning people to leave immediately. After a week of raids some 50,000 people had been killed and as many injured. Over 40,000 properties had been destroyed in the inferno caused by a mixture of incendiary and high explosive bombs. Air Marshal 'Bomber' Harris, backed by Churchill, believed that the carpet-bombing of cities such as Hamburg and Dresden would shorten the war by destroying the morale of the German people. They believed this strategy would save the lives of thousands of Allied troops. They were wrong. Just as the Nazi bombing raids on Britain had stiffened upper lips, the onslaught from the skies only hardened the determination of the civilian population to fight on.

It was in Hamburg that I underwent one of the most moving musical experiences of my life – a performance of Beethoven's Ninth Symphony. I had never heard this majestic work before and, incorporating as it does Schiller's *Ode to Joy*, it seemed that evening to embody the hopes we had that a better Europe might emerge from the chaos of war. As I left the concert hall and headed for the Atlantic Hotel's long bar, I felt as though my feet were off the ground. The symphony later became the anthem of the movement for a unified Europe. By 2011, the European Community was to be dominated economically by a unified, successful and, as ever, disciplined Germany.

I had one more examination to take to complete my inter-BSc (Economics). The subject was Logic and the place chosen for the test was Hamburg, to where I was given a lift on a Friday. I spent the Saturday and Sunday swotting in my room in a small hotel not far from the Four Seasons. On Sunday evening, I reckoned I had earned a treat so wandered along

92

to my favourite watering hole. I had planned for a good meal and an early night but as I entered the grand foyer, I encountered two young lieutenants from my unit on seventy-two-hour passes. They planned to spend the evening in the famous cocktail bar. Persuading me to join them, we sat around the bar eating Roquefort sandwiches and drinking White Ladies – gin, lemon juice and Cointreau. The combination was literally explosive. Having staggered back to my hotel I collapsed on the bed. If I opened my eyes the room spun round. Before I could even get to the washbasin I was horribly sick. Much of the night was spent cleaning up the mess. It was not the ideal way to prepare for an exam in Logic.

As I entered the examination room on Monday morning, hangover written clearly on my ashen face, the supervising officer looked sympathetic. With a shaky hand I started to write and somehow completed the questions. Perhaps the examining authorities decided to be kind with the marking that summer? In due course I was informed I had passed. A celebration was called for – but not with White Ladies.

During my athletics sojourn in Hamburg I had met an Airborne captain nicknamed 'Red' – a reference to his hair rather than politics. A once tough, now rather overweight, hard-drinking hell-raiser, his duties seemed to leave him with a lot of spare time. To help him spend it, he had an equally hard-drinking blonde buxom member of the British Control Commission as his girlfriend. I had told Red that I had met a young German woman in Oldenburg named Karen and he suggested that we should all go for a long weekend to a resort on the Baltic coast named Travemünde. What better way of celebrating my success?

Karen was delighted at the prospect of a holiday, however short. As for my driver Hans, he cheekily asked if he could bring his girlfriend, too. I requested a seventy-two-hour pass and off we set in a Volkswagen, to meet up with Red on the coast. On the way we stayed one night at a B&B farmhouse. It smelt strongly of animals and was short of hot water – but this could not dampen Hans' high spirits. He asked a special favour; instead of the girls sharing one room and us the other, could he sleep with his girlfriend? My Karen was a well-brought-up eighteen-year-old virgin and the extent of our lovemaking was far short of sharing a bed. To reassure her that I would not take advantage of the arrangement, or her, I undertook to draw a line down the length of the room between our two narrow beds. Like a true officer and gentleman I promised that I would not cross the line during the night. Lying in my bed in the dark I heard the rustle of clothes as she undressed and then felt a kiss on my cheek. That was as far as it went. Hans, no doubt, enjoyed more activity.

At Travemünde, however, I found events more exciting. There Karen had her own room but, as we all sat on the sand in the warm night air with the Baltic lapping gently on the beach, Red proposed that we have a swim. No one had a bathing costume so we all stripped off and made a dash for the sheltering sea. I had never before seen a naked woman – except in Old Master paintings and sculpture. Now three confronted me. I was thankful that, unlike the Trojan hero Paris, I did not have to choose which of the three beauties deserved an apple.

Back at base in Oldenburg, activity increased sharply as relations between Russia and the West reached crisis pitch. Under the post-war agreement between the victorious allies, Berlin had been included in the Russian zone of occupation. Each of the Western powers had an area of control within the former German capital however and access to the city through Soviet-controlled Eastern Germany. To test the nerve of the West, Russia suddenly forbade the passage of people and supplies through its zone. Moscow, in effect, imposed a blockade on the city.

Was this the overture to the Third World War? Moscow had an agenda for aggressive expansion – the Communist take on imperialism. Were Russia's leaders, namely Stalin, lunatic enough to risk plunging their recently-ravaged country into a major conflict with their erstwhile allies – one that could now, with the development in armaments, easily tip into nuclear holocaust? This was the newborn nightmare. How far would they push their luck? The Anglo-American response to the Berlin blockade would set the thermometer for decades of chilly standoff.

Despite growing international tension I was allowed to take some leave and chose a holiday camp in the American Army sector in Bavaria near the German-Austrian border. It was my good fortune to be accompanied by another junior officer, John Parkes, a most convivial companion, who was waiting to train at London's Guy's Hospital as a doctor. We had a great time, clambering up the lower slopes of mountains overshadowed by the mighty Zugspitze; wining and dining in the Americans' Garmisch nightclub; and visiting local sights such as Oberammergau, scene of the famous Passion Play re-enactment of the crucifixion. There was great excitement in the small town. The local people were busy rehearsing for the first production of the play since the war.

We were in the land once ruled by crazy King Ludwig, best known for his neo-Gothic monument to his idol Richard Wagner and the gods and creatures of German mythology – the fantastical fairyland Neuschwanstein Castle, perched high above the Forggensee Lake in the foothills of the Alps. We did not visit that monumental folly but toured the smallest of Ludwig's three palaces, the charming Rococo Linderhof. Inspired by the Petit Trianon at Versailles, it has a Venus Grotto where the King and his favoured guests were ferried about in a golden swan boat.

Meanwhile, more and more troops arrived at our depot to

draw vehicles in preparation for a possible Russian onslaught. The American and British Air Forces flew supplies into the beleaguered city in what became known as the Berlin Airlift. As tension increased, the British Government decided to halt the demobilisation of national servicemen due for release in the late summer and autumn. The only exception made was for those who had been accepted by universities for the autumn term. I was one of the lucky ones. On the morning of my departure from Oldenburg, I called at the flat where Karen lived with her war-widowed mother. We kissed goodbye in the doorway and I promised to keep in touch. Within two years, she was married to a Control Commission official.

On my return to war-ravaged London I found the blitzed capital basking in the glow of the hugely successful Olympic Games it had hosted a month before – from 29 July to 14 August. Mounted in less than two years on a slender budget, the 1948 Games were good for the reputation and morale of my old school Wanstead High, as Geoffrey Elliot, one of a number of fine young athletes it produced at that time, represented Britain in the pole vault.

The school's policy of employing top athletes as trainers had paid off. The school had won every available athletics trophy in the eastern counties over several years. It had also produced a nigh-unbeatable rugby team.

Some four thousand athletes from fifty-nine nations had gathered in London for the great post-war event – held against a background of global tensions. In Germany, there was the Soviet blockade of Berlin; Czechoslovakia had been gobbled up by the aggressive communist expansion; the Cold War was underway. The Soviet Union had never been part of the Olympic movement but this time it tried to send a team of weight-lifters. In Greece, birthplace of the games, a vicious civil war was raging. the creation of the State of Israel had sparked the conflict with neighbouring Arab states that continues to this day. Germany and Japan, understandably, were not invited to take part.

Women had made an enormous contribution in bringing about the defeat of Hitler and his allies, yet they made up less than ten per cent of the competitors in the games. One of them, however, became a superstar, winning four gold medals in athletics. She was Fanny Blankers-Koen, thirty-year-old mother of two from the Netherlands.

The austerity Olympics, overshadowed as they were by post-war economic problems and shortages, were a great success, and ended with their honour restored after the blatant racism of the previous 1936 Berlin games. That summer of 1948, Britain reinstalled the virtues for which the event had been created. We came low on the medals board, coming twelfth with twenty-three, only three of which were gold. But, in recognition of 'good effort', we got an award for careful husbandry and efficiency and a profit on the great show of £29,000.

What a contrast to London's 2012 Olympiad. After seven years of preparation, and at considerable cost at a time of economic crisis, Britain was rewarded with a great haul of medals and an enhanced reputation for impressive organisation on a massive scale. Our athletes had been helped to perform so well by the system of Lottery funding for training set up by John Major when briefly Chancellor of the Exchequer in 1989-90. But politicians generally have been guilty of neglecting sport for decades, treating it all too often as a luxury disposable extra. By August 2012, for example, the Coalition Government had approved the sale of 21 state school playing fields. Roughly a third of Britain's gold medals were won by athletes educated in private schools. Sadly, very few state schools had followed the example of Wanstead High, which in the far-off, war-ravaged 1940s had employed top athletics trainers to such good effect.

Within a week of returning home to Leytonstone I entered the London School of Economics, better known as the LSE, the 'ungodly institution in Houghton Street', off the Aldwych. To save money, I lived at home rather than in a students' hostel. This was not ideal for getting the most out of university life but money was in short supply. Still, having volunteered for the army in 1946, I did receive a reasonably generous ex-serviceman's education grant.

Founded by Sidney and Beatrice Webb, together with R.H. Tawney and William Beveridge, the school had close links with the Labour Government of the day. Both Prime Minister Attlee and Chancellor of the Exchequer Hugh Dalton had taught there. But the person whose presence gave the school the reputation of being a left-wing nest of socialists was Professor Harold Laski. Regarded by many as the foremost socialist thinker in the West, he attracted press attention when, as Chairman of the Labour Party during the 1945 General Election, some of his ill-judged comments had prompted Attlee to declare; 'A period of silence from you would be welcome.'

Silence was the last thing his adoring students at the LSE wanted from him. He truly was a great teacher. The university had been founded to promote subjects close to the hearts of Fabian socialists.

With a view to one day specialising in foreign affairs as a journalist, I had chosen International Relations as the special subject for my degree. Although the respected academic Noel Annan had observed that the LSE, with Oxford and Cambridge, was one of the three sources of intellectual excitement in modern Britain, it was very different in style and appearance from the two old universities. The drab Houghton Street building could have been that of an inner-city polytechnic, lacking in architectural distinction. There were no dreaming spires, no manicured lawns, no oak-panelled dining halls, no punting on the Thames. It was a depressing environment and not conducive to studying on campus.

In his contribution to *My LSE*, a collection of essays by former alumni, Chaim Bermant (postgraduate student from 1955-57), is scathing about his experience; 'My first shock was the building itself, a charmless pile, like the head-office of a minor insurance company, hidden away in a back street ... the immediate feeling was one of constriction amounting almost to a sense of imprisonment, especially between lectures, when one could be trampled under-foot by the swirling crowds in the narrow corridors.'

On my first day, I sat in a rather chilly room with about twenty other undergraduates to be welcomed by Professor Charles Manning, Head of the International Relations Department – a frail, ascetic-looking man whose pure white hair added to his air of academic distinction. South African by birth, he had been a Rhodes Scholar at Oxford following distinguished service in the First World War, graduating from Brasenose College with a double first in Law. In 1930 he became the Burton Professor of International Relations at the LSE. Despite his expertise in International Law he did not base his lectures on the subject, nor on International History, which was the other obvious approach. His ambition was to get International Relations accepted as an independent academic discipline in its own right. His interest in abstruse German philosophy shone through his teaching and it was the German-Jewish students in our group who understood him best. To make matters more difficult, he had not written any books explaining his approach to the subject. Some of us floundered until rescued by more down-to-earth lecturers.

Due to my extra-mural studies while in the army, I was

ahead of other students of my age in the department. At nineteen I had been demobilised having completed the first year of my degree course. I had three years in which to do two years' work and I decided to spend part of my 'spare' time doing an evening course in shorthand and typing at a nearby Pitman's Commercial College. My main objective was not to win a first class degree but to prepare myself to be a journalist and, with hope, get a job on a newspaper as soon as I graduated. I also joined the Art and Labour Societies, and the Rugby Club. Although they were not part of my course, I attended lectures on Government by Laski, too. The lecture hall was always packed for those. He seemed to speak spontaneously, without notes, relying on his extraordinary memory, his words laced with wit. At the end of each lecture, students would rush to the library to get the books he had recommended.

My own privilege of listening to Laski was short-lived. He died in March 1950. Students for whom his book-lined study had been an open house wept at their loss. Lionel Robbins, Professor of Economics, did not weep. There had been a noticeable chilliness – no doubt largely political – in his relationship with Laski. Yet some of it may have been professional jealousy. Although a brilliant and cultured man, Robbins' lectures were ponderous compared to Laski's and wartime Cabinet Office work had inflated his air of self-importance that did not endear him to some of his students. On Laski, Robbins had once commented bitchily; 'However clever he appeared to be, it seemed to me that there was a slightly ersatz quality about much of his thinking.'

To the horror of the left-wing students, Laski was replaced by Professor Michael Oakeshott, a Conservative political philosopher. They rightly saw it as a deliberate move to end the school's reputation as a hotbed of socialism.

During my first term at the LSE I earned the displeasure

of Professor Manning by choosing to produce for a seminar a paper on Commonwealth Relations, in which I criticised the racial policies of South Africa. In those early days I had not realised that he was such an active apologist for the policies of his own country and, indeed, from 1964 he became Chairman of the South Africa Society. Normally a courteous man, he was curt and sarcastic when I read my paper and as I walked away from the seminar I felt humiliated and depressed. Then someone took me by the arm. It was Frank Chambers, one of the lecturers, who said that he had very much enjoyed my paper. He told me he was involved in writing a book on International Affairs from 1914 onwards and would be grateful if I might allow him to use what I had written to cover the Commonwealth section. I would receive an acknowledgement in the foreword, he assured me. In a moment my depression was transformed into euphoria. What a breakthrough! This, I thought, was bound to impress an editor when I applied for a job.

In March 1950, the 1000-page book appeared – *This Age of Conflict* by Chambers, Christina Phelps Harris and Charles Bayley. There, in the preface, grateful acknowledgement for help was briefly given to a list of people including Professor Manning and some members of his staff – Geoffrey Goodwin and Brian Tunstall. Singled out for special mention, however, was Mr A.W. Butler, for giving permission to use a paper of his on the British Commonwealth 'which appears almost without alteration'. What a snub for Manning! Did the kindly Frank Chambers realise this? He never gave any indication if so, not even when I visited him at home in Putney.

It was during my first term at the LSE that Caroline Offley Shore – Lina – came back into my life in a helpful way. As the widow of an Indian Army general, she had been delighted when I was accepted for an officer cadetship in that famous force and shared my disappointment when I was obliged to

101

transfer to the British Army. During a visit to my grandmother at Lina's apartment in the Clock Tower at Hampton Court Palace, she called me in to see her. On learning that I had decided to become a journalist she asked if I would like to meet Desmond MacCarthy, the distinguished literary critic of *The Sunday Times* who lived nearby at Garrick's Villa, Hampton, once owned by the eighteenth-century actor David Garrick. I was delighted at the thought of making such a contact and through his wife Mary, an appointment was made for me to visit in January 1949. Foolishly, I failed to do research on him before the visit and arrived assuming that Desmond would have Conservative leanings. I quickly discovered how wrong that was.

Born in 1877, part Irish, part French, part German, this charming, urbane, liberal man had been in the forefront of the battle to tackle social injustice and win a better deal for the have-nots. He was pleased that I had chosen to study at the LSE and talked about the Webbs and their efforts to improve social conditions. Did I read the *New Statesman*? When I confessed that I bought *The Economist* and read the *Statesman* when I could find a free copy, he smiled and nodded in an understanding way. Then he revealed that as a young man he had written for the *Statesman*, which was 'out to right the wrongs of the world'. In those days, the Webbs were directors of the paper – as was George Bernard Shaw who had encouraged Desmond to become its dramatic critic. Did I read Shaw? By luck I had recently read *Arms and the Man*. He clearly had a very high regard for Shaw and urged me to read more when I could find time. And what about Keynes? Here again I was in luck as I was currently reading his *Economic Consequences of the Peace*.

The economist John Maynard Keynes, eloquent and forceful advocate of the theory of full employment, was well known to Desmond from Cambridge and what was to become known as the Bloomsbury Group. As I was soon to find out, others in that intellectual clique included Leonard Woolf, writer, publisher and influential figure in the Labour Movement; his wife, novelist Virginia; biographer, Lytton Strachey; and artists Duncan Grant, Vanessa Bell and Roger Fry. Henry Lamb, another painter, was on the fringe of the group, and a painting by him hung in the MacCarthys' large and comfortable first-floor drawing room. Clive Bell, the wealthy art critic, was another associated with the incestuous bohemians.

Some of the group's links were forged during their Cambridge University days. Desmond had been at Trinity College, graduating in 1898, and while there became a member of the famous society The Apostles, having a carefully chosen, restricted membership of twelve. They were supposedly dedicated to the pursuit of truth and good causes. While acting as the society's Secretary, Lytton Strachey discovered that, according to the archives, one of its traditions was 'higher sodomy'. Graduates could continue to belong to the society but were then known as Angels. Other members during Desmond's time included Keynes, Bertrand Russell and historian G.M. Trevelyan. Several of the group were conscientious objectors during the First World War. Although aged thirty-seven when hostilities began, Desmond volunteered for service with the Red Cross, becoming an ambulance driver and stretcher-bearer.

Hearing that I had only recently completed my two years' national service, he asked me how I had enjoyed it – and we agreed that I was lucky to have missed the war, and in view of the bloodshed in India, lucky again not to have gone there as originally planned. His time on the Western Front had been an appalling experience, carrying wounded and the mangled bodies of the dead that oozed from a sea of mud. He transported them on rutted tracks to the hospitals at Ypres and other shell-racked towns behind the lines. Eventually, he was transferred to the Royal Naval Volunteer Reserve and served as a Lieutenant in Naval Intelligence at the Admiralty.

We talked a little more about my activities at the LSE and when I told him I had joined the Labour Society, he recalled how he had reported on the Labour Congress held at Central Hall, Westminster in 1917, attended by pioneers of the movement such as Will Thorne, Ben Tillett and Henderson. As a member of the Art Society too, I had been asked at the last meeting to suggest names of people who might be prepared to speak. I asked him if he might give a talk but he explained that asthma made it difficult for him to take on speaking engagements. Finally, as I was about to leave, he pointed to a chess set on a nearby table and asked me if I played. When I answered that I did not, he said I should find time to learn. A week or so later, a chess set arrived for me by post from Garrick's Villa, with a note saying he looked forward to a game one day.

There was a Chess Club at the LSE whose chairman was a certain John Stonehouse who, as a would-be politician, was active in the Labour Society. Indeed, his parliamentary ambitions dictated most of his moves and the fact that at times he adopted the slightly stooped stance of an elder statesman won him the nickname 'Lord John'. A student named Bernard Levin was secretary of the club and he and Stonehouse became close friends – and remained so until Stonehouse died. As I was not attracted to student politics I did not get to know him well until he eventually entered the Commons in the 1950s. Even before he left the LSE he had begun to earn a reputation as a dodgy financial operator. One of his sidelines was to organise student tours to East European countries and some who went complained that the currency deals he carried out on their behalf left them with less cash than they believed they should have had. Then later, when he was in charge of an official student touring organisation, there were complaints that some who had paid deposits for tours did not get them returned if the trip was cancelled. My friend Alf Morris, the late Lord Morris of Manchester, told me how as chairman of the Labour League of Youth and an executive member of the International Union of Socialist Youth, these complaints were brought to his attention. He phoned Stonehouse several times to ask about specific cases and, getting no satisfactory explanation, he eventually turned up at Stonehouse's office in London. He challenged him that he had several disgruntled students wanting their money back. Stonehouse shuffled through some files but in each case failed to provide an explanation. Putting on an air of bafflement he shrugged his shoulders and asked Alf; 'Well, what do we do now?'

'I don't know what you are going to do,' replied Alf sharply, 'but I am going to close you down!'

Stonehouse looked stunned while a short, bespectacled man who had been sitting in the office throughout the confrontation gasped; 'You can't do that to Big John!'

It was Bernard Levin.

'Oh yes I can!' said Alfred – and he did.

Bernard, in fact, won fame in his own right at the LSE. Elections to the committee of the Students' Union had become a ritual farce. Provided a candidate claimed to belong to the student societies favoured by the voters, he or she could win a place – although they were not actually known to the voters. The Labour Society was much favoured in this respect and the committee was Labour-dominated. There was a procedure for the proposer of a candidate to introduce him or her with a short supporting speech to a meeting of the Students' Union – but many never bothered to attend those sessions. As the time approached for the next elections, Bernard Levin proposed an undergraduate named Harvey Marshall and his qualifications were listed on the Student Union notice board. These included the 'fact' that the Labour Society had included him on its list of approved candidates. On the evening allotted for introducing Marshall to the students, Bernard appeared on the platform to apologise for the fact that his candidate was indisposed. According to Bernard, however, he was an excellent fellow – and he was duly elected. He was then supposed to make his victory appearance alongside the other successful candidates. Bernard appeared on the platform again with yet another apology – Harvey Marshall, he explained, did not exist. An embarrassing light had been shone on the way in which students were failing to do a proper check on those running for office. Suddenly we woke up to the fact that there was a play running in London about a large white rabbit that lived in the imagination of an alcoholic character – a rabbit named Harvey. Soon after this, the right wing took control of the union, though that had not been Bernard's intention. I had not voted for Harvey and while I occasionally met Bernard at various society functions I did not get to know him well until the late 1950s, when he was fast becoming known as one of Britain's finest journalists.

Educated first at Christ's Hospital School, Bernard chose to go on to the LSE because he nursed political ambitions. These aspirations drew him to John Stonehouse, already an active chairman of the Labour Society, and this led to their joint steerage of the Chess Club. Bernard then decided that journalism would be a more suitable career for him than politics. After a part-time job with the BBC, he started writing for *Truth* magazine – his stepping-stone to Fleet Street and fame. I came to admire Bernard not only for his skill as a writer but, eventually, for his loyalty to Stonehouse. Following the politician's disgrace, Bernard visited him in prison and remained in touch until he died.

Not content with helping me to organise my career, Lina moved in on my social life. For years she had been an active member of the English-Speaking Union, a well-connected organisation established to promote understanding and co-operation between the British and North American peoples. The US State Department and the CIA smiled benevolently on its generously-funded activities. In London it was housed in two expensive buildings in exclusive Charles Street, Mayfair. At one of my meetings with Lina in the autumn of 1948, she asked if I would be interested in joining the ESU as it was on a drive to recruit young people. She was keen to propose me for membership and offered to pay my first year's subscription. I accepted her invitation to visit the club so Mother and I met her for tea in the ornately-panelled room on the first floor. With Lina's patronage, joining was a mere formality and soon I was enrolled in the club's heavily-subsidised younger members' group. On my first visit to one of the functions, I was welcomed by a beautiful, vivacious young woman who was chairing the group – Isobel Maclean-Harris. A few years later she married another club member, John Copeman, and they remained close friends of mine until they died.

I was soon involved in a round of debates, Sunday evening dances and parties galore. In the summer there were idyllic swimming parties, and punting on the Thames. Among the members was a colourful and extrovert young Liberal, dressed like a dandy, who introduced himself as Jeremy Thorpe. In due course he came to lead his party. Another up-and-coming politician who crossed my path during my days in the ESU was Denis Healey, who was to be elected Labour MP for Leeds South East in 1952. He was previously Secretary of the Labour Party's International Department. The younger members' group sponsored an essay competition on a topic of international affairs and Healey was invited to judge it. I won.

Years later I attended a memorial meeting for an American CIA agent who had enjoyed extraordinary success infiltrating the right-wing leadership of the Labour Party and Trade Union

Movement. I mingled there with prominent Labour politicians who had turned up to pay their respects to the late Joe Godson. I had been introduced to Godson by former Labour MP Alan Lee Williams, who became Director-General of the ESU from 1979-86. He had worked harder than any other Westminster politician at trying to strengthen Britain's alliance with the USA and her role in NATO. An influential operator, he served for a time as Parliamentary Private Secretary to the Secretary of State for Defence and chaired the Parliamentary Labour Party's Defence Committee from 1976-79 when he lost his seat in the general election.

Meanwhile, back at the LSE, I agreed to be Secretary of the Rugby Club and President of the Art Society, one of the least well-attended student groups. I decided to try to boost attendance by painting eye-catching posters to advertise meetings and by getting some 'big names' to address us. There was an explosion of interest in ballet in the late 1940s, particularly among young people – and one reason for this was the writing of the author and critic Arnold Haskell. His success in popularising and explaining the art was enormous and when he accepted my invitation to speak, I knew I had a crowd-puller. He had started writing regularly on ballet for the *Daily Telegraph* some fifteen years before – the first such appointment by a British newspaper. His book *Ballet*, published by Penguin just before the Second World War, was a best-seller. He was in his late forties, trim and dapper, when he came to talk and he quickly engaged the student audience – overflowing from the packed room – by recalling that while at Westminster School he and John Gielgud, the actor, had devised a system for dodging classes to attend matinée shows including Diaghilev and Pavlova ballets. In 1922 he even met Diaghilev in Paris, thanks to Alicia Markova. By the time he addressed us he had been appointed Director of the newly-formed Sadler's Wells Ballet School, later to become the Royal Ballet School, and had introduced the word 'balletomania' into the English language. He expressed to us his huge admiration for Ninette de Valois and all she had achieved at Sadler's Wells. He was clearly excited that now ballet – some twenty years before seen as a rather precious pastime designed to entertain the few – had been taken up by the 'man in the street'. It was important, he urged, that we should allow dancers to improve by growing our knowledge of ballet and so apply high critical standards to the art.

My mother had sparked my interest in ballet by recounting how my grandmother Alice had taken her in her late teens to see the ethereal Russian ballerina Anna Pavlova dance in London during one of her exhausting freelance world tours following the First World War. Mother vividly remembered Pavlova's extraordinary and breathtaking interpretation of the *Dying Swan* – the most celebrated piece in her repertoire, performed to the melancholy music of Saint-Saens that entered the record collection of anyone who owned a gramophone.

The Haskell talk was a great success and put the Art Society on the map. An even bigger event was to follow. A young Italian student approached me to ask whether I would be interested in chairing a meeting for his uncle who was due to visit London shortly – his uncle, who happened to be Giorgio de Chirico. The most famous Italian painter of the twentieth century, in 1949 de Chirico had been elected as an Honorary Associate of The Royal Society of British Artists and it had invited him to exhibit a hundred paintings at its London headquarters. A date for his address was fixed and when my poster advertising the meeting appeared on the notice board, it created so much interest that it was agreed a larger room should be provided to accommodate the crowd. The great surrealist was sixty-two when he came to address us at the LSE and appeared frail – although he lived for almost another thirty years. His opinions, however, were strong and delivered with vigour. As he needed an interpreter, his nephew took the chair at the meeting and we were delighted to see that the Director of the School, Sir Alexander Carr-Saunders, was in the audience, together with other members of the staff. Sir Alexander, who was deeply interested in painting, had been known to complain that the LSE was a colony of philistines. Now he made known his pleasure that at last it could find time for art.

As it happened, de Chirico's visit took place when he was still brooding over his experience with the controversial Exhibition of Metaphysical Painting, held at the 1948 Venice Biennale. He was upset because, in his opinion, the organisers wrongly spread the belief that Mussolini's regime had forced Italian artists to paint to convention instead of being allowed freedom of expression. He maintained he had suffered no constraint. He made known, too, that he had a poor opinion of 'modern painting' that he complained was totally lacking in technical ability. Although the Venice exhibition had been arranged to glorify his work he thought it was unbalanced, concentrating on one of his painting styles only. The last straw was that a fake de Chirico had been included – and, in his view, a very obvious fake. He was touchy about the large number of counterfeits finding their way onto the market and even made a joke about my poster that incorporated his style. I had been inspired by his famous work of 1913, *The Uncertainty of the Poet* (now in the Tate Gallery), painted in tribute to the poet and critic Guillaume Appollinaire. At least I had not signed it 'de Chirico'!

He was, of course, best known for his dreamlike pictures of ghostly streets and squares, of colonnades and broken classical statuary, of long shadows and steam trains (he was the son of a railway engineer). His use of long perspectives and odd combinations of objects influenced Salvador Dali and other surrealist painters. I learned later that he had sometimes perversely denounced as forgeries some of his genuine early works.

Soon after the meeting Carr-Saunders invited the officers of the Art Society to supper in his private room. A rather stern, saturnine-looking man, he had studied biology and law. He made an important contribution in the field of resources, population and demography. Before we sat down he congratulated us on the success of the society and regretted the fact that the LSE neglected art in its choice of subjects. He shared my opinion of the depressing nature of the LSE building; he thought it looked more like an office block, whilst I thought it resembled a cheaply-built suburban polytechnic. The meal itself, however, was less relaxed. He slurped disconcertingly loudly as he tucked into his soup and then proceeded to test our knowledge of painting in a 'cat and mouse' session, revealing his irritation when we failed to recognise some Flemish and Dutch paintings on the wall.

My speciality was the field of early English watercolours. As a hard-up student, wandering around London galleries I was sometimes tempted to calculate how many days I would have to starve in order to buy, say, a satirical work by Thomas Rowlandson. In those days, around 1950, they were not so expensive. But by the time I was earning a reasonable salary prices had soared, due in part to buying up by Americans, in particular Paul Mellon. The tycoon had fallen for early British painting and went on to found the Yale Centre for British Art in 1977.

In 2007 a selection of masterpieces from the Yale Centre went on show at London's Royal Academy of Art and the expert chosen to write up the show for their magazine was Giles Waterfield. I had got to know Giles when as a young man he had been appointed director of the Dulwich Picture Gallery. He had met Mellon when an exhibition from Dulwich was lent to the National Gallery of Art in Washington. Giles wrote that Mellon belonged to the Medici tradition; 'a man of enormous wealth, buying for the whole of a long adulthood. Where he differed from the Medici was that he did not engage in personal display ... he embodied the old-fashioned notion of a gentleman ... Restraint, good manners based on consideration for others, avoidance of self-promotion; these were all characteristics he exemplified.'

On learning more about him, I decided that if I could choose to inhabit the earth as someone else it would be as Mr Mellon.

My newfound prestige as Art Society President and poster painter was soon to be tarnished. A meeting was planned to provide a platform for the editors of some struggling literary magazines. The title chosen was 'Little Reviews' but when my poster appeared it advertised instead a meeting on 'Little Revues'! The society's Secretary, an attractive well-read girl named Barbara Knott, hissed in disbelief when we met in the cafeteria; 'You spelt "Review" wrong!'

My solecism, however, helped to keep up attendance. A goodly number turned up anticipating a survey of current satirical political or burlesque shows. There were some giggles as I apologised for the misleading title and I noticed a disappointed exodus at the back.

A short walk from the LSE, across Lincoln's Inn Fields, stands one of the most extraordinary museums in the world. Created by the famous Regency architect Sir John Soane (1753-1837) – who designed the Bank of England – it is a run of several houses converted by him to provide a home for himself and his valuable collection of artefacts. Packed with pieces of classical and Egyptian sculpture and pottery, it has a clever system of display where paintings are hung on hinged panels, revealing yet more behind when they are swung open.

Barbara Knott, recovered from the typographical *faux pas*, invited the director of the Sir John Soane Museum to address the Art Society. The scholarly aesthete John Summerson was delighted to get the opportunity to talk about his, at that time, little-known treasure trove. Summerson was rather haughty and aristocratic in appearance and he had a dry sense of humour that appealed to the students who got to know him. He had founded the Georgian Group in 1937 to protect Georgian buildings from destruction. Appointed as curator of the Soane Museum in 1945, his top priority was to reunite the collection that had been dispersed for safety during the war. He achieved this and the museum reopened to the public once more in 1947.

I came to know and love the place with its eerie, antiquated atmosphere and was to become involved with another of Soane's buildings – the Dulwich Picture Gallery, the first public art gallery in the country, that he designed. For some years I sat on the committee, raising funds and organising events to safeguard what is one of the finest collections of old master paintings in Britain.

In my mission to impress newspaper editors I saw a notice concerning the Royal Asiatic Society's annual universities' essay prize. The subject was 'Turkey; Stepping Stone to India' and I decided to enter the competition. With help from an LSE geopolitics lecturer named Turnstall and an expert at the Royal Institute of International Affairs named Kirk, I won the grand prize of £30, a mention in *The Times* and a certificate, presented at the rather dusty, old-fashioned headquarters of the society in West London.

If I had been a dutiful son I would have offered the money to my parents to help towards my upkeep. Instead, I spent it on travelling to Europe during the long summer vacation of 1950. My, as ever, generous and indulgent parents encouraged the plan. At the same time, the University of Bonn was offering a week's course for undergraduates as part of the West German Government's propaganda campaign to prove that their citizens, so soon after the defeat of the Nazis, were an invaluable part of democratic Europe which should be seriously considering some form of federal organisation. My two closest friends in the International Relations Department were Ronald Brandon – known to my old school chum Alan Barton – and David Elliot, who would have a distinguished Civil Service career culminating as Secretary to the Council of Ministers of the European Union, and eventually received a KCMG Knighthood to add to his well-earned CB (Companion of the Order of the Bath).

We three agreed to sign up for the Bonn course and, from there, to hitchhike through Switzerland, Italy and France. I proposed we should visit Venice and see the 1950 Biennale – an event I learnt about from de Chirico. In my mind we were about to embark upon the equivalent of the Grand Tours so fashionable for upper-class young Englishmen in the eighteenth and nineteenth centuries. By the 1780s, some 40,000 classically-educated tourists were crossing the Alps to view the cultural glories of Florence, Venice, Naples and Rome.

En route for Bonn we decided to visit Paris and stayed in a youth hostel on the outskirts of the city. I had already started my love affair with the French capital, having travelled there with the LSE rugby team in the spring of 1949. Over a long weekend we played against our hosts, the renowned Haute Ecole Commercial. The French students did their best to undermine our training with wine and late nights. As well as conducting us to that symbol of French glory, the Arc de Triomphe, and sending us up the Eiffel Tower, they led us into the red-light district of Pigalle for a comprehensive tour of its strip clubs and bars. On one night, eight of us, sweaty and goggle-eyed, crammed into a small upstairs room in a street off the sex-for-sale Boulevard de Clichy for a private 'exhibition' by two ladies who had known better times. There was much haggling about the fee and eventually we staggered off noisily down the stairs more disenchanted than debauched.

We had more fun when we were taken to the Lido nightclub on the Champs-Elysées to see one of its famously erotic topless plumed spectaculars. As we approached the club our student guide got into conversation with four women loitering nearby. He explained to us that the Lido did not allow single women in the door, to prevent prostitutes using the club to pick up clients. If we agreed to escort them in they would pay for the first expensive round of drinks, such as allowed one to stay for the show. No arm-twisting was required and as soon as we were seated and the drinks bought, the girls moved off in search of punters.

For a cheap lunch, we went to the cavernous Chartier restaurant at the end of an alley off one of the great boulevards. It was popular with students on a budget. There we tackled chewy steaks and *pommes frites* washed down with carafes of red wine as hectic waiters scooted around us, balancing their laden trays above our heads. It was rumoured the steaks were really horsemeat, and that's how they kept prices so low.

On first entering Chartier, designed and built in the grand Parisian style, I assumed it had been an upper-class eatery that had slipped down in the world. But this great value establishment had been opened with the original intention of catering to working-class people and hard-up students such as us. It was run, and still is to this day, on simple lines – first come, first seated, no reservations taken, fast turnover. Customers share a table with whoever turns up. Loitering is not encouraged. No sooner have you taken your last mouthful than the bill is quickly scrawled on the paper tablecloth. My mock Toulouse

Lautrec drawings of hook-nosed toffs in curly-brimmed top hats were whisked away by the unappreciative waiter. A pristine new sheet instantly replaced my potentially priceless work of art.

Our short visit to Paris had gone well and the Germans made a great fuss of us when we arrived in Bonn. Located on the Rhine near France and The Netherlands, it had been chosen as the temporary seat of government of the Federal Republic of Germany in 1947. The sleepy provincial town had suddenly sprouted parliament and civil service buildings as well as foreign embassies. Once, as the seat of the Prince-Archbishops of nearby Cologne, it had played a key role in the Holy Roman Empire. Now at last it regained an *entrée* to the power game. At seminars in the university or around the lunch and dinner tables, we found there was wistful talk of the days when Europe was unified under the Emperor Charlemagne in the misty ninth century. From the Ebro to the Elbe, people had enjoyed peace, order and Christian culture. Little mention was made of Germany's recent attempt to unify Europe under the Nazi flag.

One day we visited Cologne, once the largest city in Rome's northern empire. We saw the great Gothic cathedral rising from an area severely damaged by the Allied bombers, putting an end to Hitler's imperial dream. On another day we cruised along the Rhine, passing hills clothed with woods and vineyards, visiting towns such as Coblenz and Linz where an oompah-pah band played on the quayside to welcome us. More uplifting music was supplied back in Bonn, the birthplace of Beethoven. From there we travelled by train on cheap student fares to Bern, the colourful and picturesque capital of Switzerland – smaller than Zurich, Geneva or Basel. We booked into a youth hostel and wandered around the narrow cobbled streets, admiring medieval towers, baroque palaces and churches. Bern got its name from the German word for 'bear' and we joined the crowd watching some disport themselves in the city's bear pit. Nearby were ornate fountains and arcades with gift shops, bars and restaurants, permeating the air with mouth-watering odours. There were platters of smoked meats, sauerkraut and fine cheeses. But our tight budget precluded sitting down for a meal. We could not even afford a chocolate bear.

Bern was to be the starting point for our hitchhiking travel but next morning David broke the news that, out of money, he was going to head home. Ron and I travelled on, sometimes separately as it was easier for one to get a lift, but always meeting up at youth hostels along the route. With a Union Jack pinned boldly to my rucksack, I had little trouble getting rides. My next stop was at Interlaken and then it was over the Alps by the St Gotthard Pass into Italy. The hostel at Lugarno had the luxury of a small swimming pool and buoyed up by that, I walked along the shore of beautiful Lake Como. Then it was on to Venice to meet up with Ron.

The Somerset man who started the craze for the Grand Tour, Mr Thomas Coryate, described Venice in 1608 as 'the most glorious and heavenly show upon the water that ever any mortal eye beheld.' I, too, was stunned by its splendour, but not so much by our youth hostel. Housed in an old nunnery on an island in the lagoon, it was infested with rats. We escaped it to wander around the main tourist areas, overcome by the glory of St Mark's and the Doge's Palace. A ride in a gondola was beyond our budget so we took the *vaporetti*, the crowded water buses that ply the main canals.

Ron and I delighted in hopping on and off the *vaporetti* as they travelled along the Grand Canal. We would plunge into the narrow, smelly tangle of streets, take a breather on the Rialto Bridge then enter the hallowed cool of the Accademia, one of Italy's finest galleries, hung with the work of Venetian artists. And then there was the Biennale, the biggest international art show in the world. Created in 1895 as part of the coronation celebrations of King Umberto of Italy, it had continued during the Second World War – but with a bias towards art the fascists found acceptable. The various national pavilions were spread around the gardens at the end of the island. In 1950, the British pavilion was displaying the sculpture of Barbara Hepworth. I had not seen her work before and was impressed.

Next stop was Florence. Ron and I arranged to rendezvous at the city's youth hostel. On arriving, we discovered it was right next door to an open-air cinema screening *Mighty Joe Young*. Joe, we came to learn, was a gorilla and his roars kept us awake until late into the night. Slightly sleepy, we wandered into the Uffizi Gallery with its supreme collection of Italian Renaissance art; gaped at Michelangelo's statue of David – symbolising the strength and independence of the city – in the Accademia Gallery; and then visited the Bargello Fortress to compare that macho marble to Donatello's turn at David. The work resurrected skills mislaid throughout the Dark Ages. It was the first freestanding bronze nude statue of significant scale completed since ancient times. The sensitive study of youth took my breath away. Produced a generation before Michelangelo's great work, I preferred it to the stone version. I preferred Florence to Venice too. Being less dependent on tourists, it was cheaper and more relaxed in its attitude to visitors. In later years, my preference matured and *La Serenissima* stole my affections.

As it was Holy Year, we imagined Rome would be bursting with pilgrims and decided to give it a miss. It was time to turn and head for home. Hitchhiking via Pisa, we stopped for a few days' rest at a hostel in lovely, secluded Lerici, in a bay near La Spezia. Suddenly I realised that in the history of English poets, this was a special place. The book I had requested as my school's Economics prize had been the Edmund Blunden biography of Percy Bysshe Shelley. A review of it had aroused my interest in the romantic poet and radical. Now I recalled that his body had been burned on a funeral pyre on the beach here. He had drowned when his yacht, the *Don Juan,* had foundered in a heavy sea. He was not quite thirty. His friend Keats died the year before, aged twenty-six, and when Shelley's body was searched a book of Keats' poems was in his coat pocket.

We were permitted to stay for three nights at the hostel above the small beach. We sunbathed and swam off the rocks with two friendly Australian girls who, like us, were on their way to France. I wished I had brought a book of Shelley's poems with me. Instead, I had packed in my rucksack Machiavelli's *The Prince* and a notebook in which I was trying to write a play in blank verse about the struggle between democratic Athens and totalitarian Sparta. This effort had been inspired by *The Peloponnesian War,* written by the fifth-century BC Greek soldier, Thucydides.

We were now approaching the stretch of Mediterranean coast that had been my mother's playground in the 1920s. I persuaded Ron that we should meet up in Monte Carlo to visit the great casino where she had sipped cocktails while watching fortunes won and lost. The journey took me through San Remo, a favourite resort of Lina's, and to Menton in France where I arrived too late to get into a hostel for the night. As dusk descended I wandered along the beach looking for a place to spread my groundsheet. Seeing some rough characters loitering, I changed plan and headed back into the town to look for a park. Instead, I found the cemetery and slept like the dead on the flat top of a large stone tomb. It was eerie but it was dry. Some fifty years later, Giles Waterfield was to add novelist to his artistic credentials, writing *The Long Afternoon* set in Menton just before and during the First World War. At that time, doctors recommended it as 'the warmest, most sheltered place in civilised Europe'.

119

No wonder I had slept so well. Giles had a link with Menton. Some generations before, his family had settled there and created the famous garden still admired today.

In Monte Carlo, although not dressed quite like the smart gambling set, we sauntered into the casino. We admired the ornate décor with its sparkling chandeliers but decided not to risk our luck at the tables. Then it was on through Nice to Cannes. The youth hostel there was in a former monastery on the Ile Sainte-Marguerite, grown about with pines, myrtle and heather that scented the air as you trod upon the foliage. The harbour was busy with yachts and stretching itself luxuriantly along the coast for a couple of miles was the world-famous promenade – La Croisette. We found the Australian girls we had met at Lerici were already installed there and assisted by one of them, I cooked up a supper of fish and tomato stew that we enjoyed with cheap red wine and baguettes.

These were the last few days of sea, sun and sand before we headed north for London. I sent a card to arrive home ahead of me, hoping it would remind Mother of her own Riviera dream. No English milord could have enjoyed his Grand Tour more than had I.

There was one other visit to Paris before I left the LSE. Two friends from schooldays, David Beadle and David Monro, persuaded me to take them on a long weekend trip to the city. Pleased to have an opportunity to show off my *savoir faire*, I whisked them around the sights – risking our lives in the stampede of traffic around the Place de la Concorde; ushering them down the gravelly paths of the Tuileries and into the Louvre where we took in the *Winged Victory of Samothrace* before reaching the *Mona Lisa*, who was patiently waiting for us. I took them to eat on the long refectory tables at Chartier. On the Left Bank we found the Rose Rouge, a jazz club with a mellow sax. We followed the trail of the more literary tourists to eat Welsh rarebit at Café Flore on the Boulevard St Germain where Simone de Beauvoir, Jean-Paul Sartre and Albert Camus had been regular customers during and just after the war. By the time we arrived it was much frequented by the existentialist disciples of Sartre, who had abandoned his upstairs room in the café by then to write in an apartment on the Place de St Germain.

I would have liked to take my chums to the renowned restaurant La Tour d'Argent on the left bank of the Seine, but I would have to wait until 1975 when a small group of wealthy Americans took me there as their guest. We dined in the upstairs room with its view across the river to Notre Dame. A small army of tail-coated waiters carried out well-drilled manoeuvres around our candle-lit table. Everyone ordered the restaurant's celebrated duck – every one served over the decades had a number. I regret I cannot recall the number of mine. But I shall never forget how it was served and savour it still. Tender slices were served first in a rich sauce followed by another plate with the legs, light and crispy, as a fine claret was served reverently by the sommelier.

I decided that to complete my man-of-the-world act, I would lead my disciples to a fashion show. For decades the dollars of wealthy American women such as Lina had supported the Parisian fashion houses. At first she bought from the House of Worth, whose clients – that included Empress Eugénie – in the late nineteenth century had been painted by Winterhalter wearing the costly silk tulle concoctions. Worth became the father of *haute couture*. My mother talked of him but even more so of Captain Molyneux, to whom Lina transferred her patronage after the First World War. His refined creations had a dignity that appealed to royalty and high society. In our crumpled sports coats and scruffy grey flannels we were not exactly dressed for the scene, but remembering the name of the *vendeuse* who looked after Lina, I herded us in the direction of the House of Molyneux.

On arriving, I told the receptionist that I was a friend of Mrs Offley Shore and would like to speak to her *vendeuse*. If possible we would like to sit in on one of the fashion shows, which at that time were still conducted in-house. It worked. The *vendeuse*, for all her practised *sang-froid*, could not suppress some stunned surprise. But Lina's name opened doors and soon we were seated on three spindly-looking gilt chairs in a high-ceilinged pearl grey salon ogling the equally surprised models, who that day were showing lingerie.

Captain Edward Molyneux MC, wounded three times in the First World War as an officer in the Duke of Wellington's Regiment, opened his fashion house in the Rue Royale on borrowed money. He declared; 'Clothes must avoid the over-dressed, the obvious, the showy; also they must wear very well.'

Fleeing from Paris a few days before the Germans occupied the city in the Second World War, he returned to resume business soon after its liberation. In 1947, however, he faced a new challenge – the House of Christian Dior launched, unveiling the delightfully feminine and controversially fabric-extravagant 'New Look'. Molyneux closed his Paris House in 1950 – soon after our visit – but he reopened it in 1964.

As we swaggered away from his showroom, having thanked the bemused *vendeuse*, I was left in no doubt that my friends saw me as the gatekeeper to glamour.

6

The Forlorn Hope

Back at the LSE in the autumn of 1950, I was nervous. Now entering my final year, I had neglected my examination subjects although I had mastered shorthand and typing, and had had a selection of material published. But I had also spent so much time in London's galleries that I would have felt more confident facing an exam on art history.

Luckily for me, a fine teacher named Martin Wight had arrived as lecturer in the International Relations Department and began to make sense of the subject for me. A specialist in modern history, he had spent time at Chatham House and Nuffield College, Oxford, and had been on the staff of *The Observer* newspaper before arriving at the LSE. He was a combination of political realist and romantic. A conscientious objector during the war, he recalled how, on Victory in Europe night, he had cycled out of Nuffield College into the Oxfordshire countryside and saw people lighting bonfires on village greens to celebrate the defeat of Nazi Germany. It brought home to him the continuity of history – for over four centuries on this same common ground people had lit fires, be they to mark the defeat of the Armada, the downfall of Napoleon or the routing of the Teutonic hordes. On the day North Korea invaded the South, he entered our lecture room ashen-faced and announced in a strained voice; 'The Third World War has begun'.

That time, mercifully, Martin's forecast was wrong, although that did not reduce my respect for him. Some students failed to share my admiration precisely because of his stance during the war. I suspected that as a result of that and being unmarried too, he perhaps felt isolated. Although physically large, he was vulnerable to ill health, and contracted jaundice. He had written a helpful book entitled *Power Politics* and introduced me to the writings of the eminent American political scientist, Professor Hans Morgenthau. As Arthur Schlesinger wrote of him; 'His masterful defence of the "national interest" as the only authentic basis for foreign policy drew effectively on the thought of the Founding Fathers and represented the culmination of the realist approach to international relations.'

I had avoided getting too deeply drawn into student politics, finding the policy and personality disputes irritating and time-wasting. News issues such as the devaluation of the pound in September 1949 further put me off, with the Tories accusing Chancellor Stafford Cripps of dishonesty for denying right up to announcement day that the government was even considering such a move. Churchill, of course, knew all too well that the Chancellor had no choice but to deny the devaluation rumours in order to avoid a disastrous run on the pound. Attlee summed up the situation thus; 'Devaluation was unavoidable. The pound was overvalued, causing extreme difficulty with the foreign exchange situation.'

But as we entered 1950, I found myself swept along by the tide of excitement generated by the imminent general election. The 1945 Parliament was nearing the end of its exciting and highly-productive life. The nation was to give its verdict on the achievements of the first majority Labour Government. Attlee decided to go to the country before holding the impending annual budget – and polling took place on 23 February, a wintry month for campaigning, especially in the North. I had done my bit for the local Leyton Labour Party and Reg Sorensen was re-elected with a comfortable majority. He was, in fact, no run-of-the-mill backbencher. His eloquent campaigning on such issues as colonial freedom made him a national figure. Indeed, at Labour's triumphant 1945 annual conference, in the contest for the seven-strong constituency section of the National Executive Committee, he had been runner-up against such 'big beasts' as Shinwell, Dalton and Morrison. Nye Bevan had come top.

Labour's total vote in the election had risen by more than 1.25 million, but its overall majority in the Commons fell from a massive 152 to a meagre 10.

Although Labour had not lost a seat in a by-election in five years, there had been a considerable redistribution of parliamentary seats – and that had done the damage. The total number of seats in east and south-east London, for example, had been cut from eighteen to nine, destroying what had been Labour strongholds.

Severely hampered by its small majority, Labour limped on in government until forced to call another General Election at the end of 1951, which returned the Tories to power.

Despite my urgent need to study I still found time to visit Desmond and Mary MacCarthy at Garrick's Villa. Mary was increasingly worried about Desmond's health but he was always generous with his time and appeared genuinely interested in my activities. When I told him I had entered for the Gladstone Memorial Essay prize, he surprised me by revealing he had heard him speak. In his opinion, Gladstone, far from being a pompous, stuffy Victorian politician, was a great enthusiast for certain causes, with a gift for communicating his moral passion to the public. Desmond had great respect for him and, comparing him favourably with some current politicians, recalled that he always demonstrated courtesy and good manners in debate.

Desmond was pleased when I revealed that I had joined the Fabian Society. A number of his friends had been active in starting it, including Bernard Shaw, who had edited Fabian essays and sat on the Executive Committee. Clifford Sharp, editor of the *New Statesman* when Desmond had first written for it, was also a Fabian. I told him that Kingsley Martin, current editor of the *NS* had recently given a talk at the LSE. Indeed, their offices were very near the school – as was my own journalistic goal, Fleet Street. In that connection I had talked to Martin Wight about my ambition and he generously offered to write to the editor of his old paper *The Observer*, recommending me for a post. I was at first tempted to accept his offer but I was not sure that I was ready to write for what was my favourite newspaper – and I did not wish to let down Martin by not being up to standard. I made enquiries with the Universities Appointments Board about training schemes for would-be journalists and was informed that the Kemsley Newspapers group had introduced one. They gave me a deadline date for applying. The scheme, in fact, had been in existence only a few years and was introduced to take the heat off Lord Kemsley when he had faced the Royal Commission on the Press, set up in 1947 by the Attlee Government.

Ministers were concerned by allegations that journalistic freedom was being choked by the concentration of newspaper ownership into the hands of a few power groups. Kemsley and Lord Beaverbrook were the two main targets. However, when Kemsley told the Royal Commission that he had an idea for training young journalists as a means of raising standards, they were delighted. It was to be known as The Kemsley Editorial Training Plan. Just in case standards didn't rise quite quickly enough, the commission recommended that a Press Council should be set up to keep an eye on them. After a delay of five years the press barons produced a toothless watchdog that did little to satisfy politicians like Aneurin Bevan, who had described the British press as 'the most prostituted in the world'.

Following the advice of the Appointments' Board, I telephoned Kemsley House to ask for an application form. To my surprise I was informed that it was too late to apply. The official told me that if I had a problem with that I should take it up with the Appointments' Board. Instead, I picked up my pen and wrote to Desmond, explained the problem and asked if he could help with a word on my behalf at the appropriate level. A letter promptly arrived from a James Fraser at Kemsley House asking me to attend for an interview. There was one vacancy still to be filled that year – on the Middlesbrough *Evening Gazette*. I got the job.

I was about to become part of the Kemsley empire, covering a great chain of provincial morning and evening papers and five national Sunday papers – *The Sunday Times, Sunday Graphic, Sunday Dispatch, Sunday Chronicle* and the *Empire News*. All but the first were to die in his hands. He also owned the *Daily Dispatch* published in Manchester but his only real national daily was *The Graphic*, sometimes entitled *The Daily Sketch*. Known as 'Lord K', he had been born Gomer Berry and was the brother of another press baron – Lord Camrose. Pompous and partial to the grander things in life, he was chauffeured around in a Rolls Royce.

Although the Kemsley scheme was designed for graduates, students were appointed before they knew the results of their final degree examinations. In my case it was just as well. I failed to pass a short commercial German language paper and my degree was postponed for a year. Foolishly, I had chosen to sit the German paper instead of opting for an easier language on the unreliable strength of the few phrases I had learned during my service with the British Army of the Rhine. I also discovered that, inappropriately, I had scored poorly in the general essay exam. The reason for that was unusual. I had fallen briefly under the influence of a talented new playwright called Christopher Fry. He had brought to the London stage a revival of verse drama. Comparisons with Shakespeare were made and the respected critic Harold Hobson of *The Sunday Times* wrote; 'He can make words dance'.

My mother, too, loved the theatre, and with her I went to see several of his plays; *The Lady's Not For Burning* (1948); *Venus Observed* (1949); and *Ring Round the Moon* (1950) – his magical translation of Anouilh's *L'Invitation au Chateau*. I was deeply impressed and affected by his style – and tried to imitate it!

Luckily, the Fry influence did not hamper my performance in the Civil Service exam for entry into the Foreign Office. Although I had no intention of joining the Diplomatic Corps, I decided that taking it would be a useful practice run for my finals. Having passed the written test I went on to the next stage. This was held over two days in a Belgravia town house where candidates were grilled in a series of interviews. Our table manners were observed as much as anything else and it seemed to be a lot about ensuring we didn't eat our peas off a knife. During an interview, I began to suspect that the questioner thought that women had had too great an influence on my life. With my father abroad for much of the war, that should hardly have been surprising.

Most of the other candidates were Oxbridge undergraduates, previously educated at public schools where they had been reared by house masters. One of my fellow LSE/high school educated candidates who did in fact score for the redbrick team to join the Foreign Office was John Morgan.

In my last year at the LSE, a policy split in the Labour Movement was precipitated by Chancellor of the Exchequer Sir Stafford 'Austerity' Cripps resigning from Attlee's government due to ill health. Hugh Gaitskell was appointed to succeed him. Cripps had recommended Gaitskell, Minister of State for Economic Affairs, as an experienced economist and Attlee accepted his advice, passing over Nye Bevan and Trade Minister Harold Wilson. It was October 1950 and the schism in the party that resulted would endure for over a decade.

Gaitskell needed a budget to meet the increase in defence expenditure resulting from the Korean War. His insistence on cuts to Bevan's baby, the National Health Service, led to the impassioned Welshman resigning from the Cabinet in April 1951, together with Wilson and John Freeman, a junior Supply Ministry minister, in April 1951. It was an issue of principle for Bevan to defend the free Health Service he had fought to set up; for Wilson, it was a calculated career move.

As I prepared for my degree examination I was dismayed to see the struggling Labour Government weakened from within. Left-wingers, disappointed by the tired administration's loss of socialist drive, now rallied to Bevan's bright red banner. So the battle lines were drawn between the 'Bevanites' and the 'Gaitskellites'. Hugh Gaitskell was to succeed Attlee as party leader in December 1955, Labour having lost power to the Tories in October 1951. In that summer, as I prepared to head for Middlesbrough, I had no idea how personally and professionally involved I would become in the war of doctrine for Labour hearts and what the serious long-term consequences of the split would be.

Before I set off for the North, a letter arrived from my friend, The Rev. Stephen Fowler. I had remained in contact with him since my time as an evacuee when he was curate of Broadwell Church. He had a holiday relief stint at an English church in Rome in August and invited me to go as his guest. But I was feeling guilty about my second-class degree, and felt that I had let my parents down. I replied to Stephen untruthfully that I was committed to start my new job immediately and suggested that he might like to invite instead my old friend from Broadwell and Wanstead, Alan Barton. Al had graduated from Exeter University and was doing national service as an officer in the RAF. He was delighted to accept Stephen's offer. Then I packed my new portable typewriter – a good luck gift from my parents – and headed for sunny Middlesbrough.

As for Desmond and Mary, I never saw them again, although we kept in touch by letter. It was characteristic of Desmond and his generous interest in the young and their ideas that, despite failing health, he made the effort that assured me a place on the Kemsley training scheme. With him busy writing and working as a leading member of the English PEN club, Mary took on the job of corresponding with me and wrote with congratulations upon my appointment.

Looking ahead, I promised my mother that I would give her a holiday, by taking her back to her old haunts in Paris, where she had not been since 1927. My father had enjoyed enough foreign travel at the taxpayer's expense during the war. Flying for the first time in our lives, our visit coincided with an appearance by the fabulous singer Lena Horne, of whom we were both great fans but had only seen in films. So we took a table at her cabaret show as well as a pew in the English church where mother's one-time lover, the English tailor, had played the organ and a drink at the luxurious Crillon Hotel where she had stayed with Lina.

My departure from Leytonstone meant my parents were able to take up an offer from a wealthy Greek couple needing live-in help. Their new employers lived in a large house in Sussex Gardens and my parents would have the self-contained basement flat and a reasonable wage. My father could continue to work at the bank and my mother could earn extra as a cook when the Greeks were entertaining. And as the controlled rent for the Leytonstone flat was so low they decided to keep the tenancy for me when, after three years training in Middlesbrough, I would return to the capital.

As for my redoubtable grandmother, she had returned to her basement flat on Walton Street after Lina died in 1956. It still had no running hot water, central heating or electricity, but the primitive conditions did not appear to depress Alice. She chain-smoked Woodbines and passed the hours playing cards, listening to her radio while fortified by bottles of stout.

On her forays to the Post Office on the Brompton Road, she resembled the ferocious old grandma in the *Sunday Express* cartoon by Giles – and young policemen offering to help her negotiate the traffic soon learned to leave her to her own devices. Over the decades she had walked along Walton Street, first as a good-looking, independent young woman on her way to chef at one of the great London houses; or heading to Hyde Park on a day off to turn heads as she rowed on the Serpentine. In the evenings, if not working, she would sometimes head for the Royal Court Theatre in nearby Sloane Square to watch Shakespeare, or head for the West End for an evening of lusty singing in a music hall. That was what her handsome brother had enjoyed when on leave from the army. An enlarged photographic portrait of him in his red regimental uniform dominated one wall of her living room until her death. A package of his letters sent from the Boer War front in South Africa were found tied in ribbon in a drawer in her bedroom (see epilogue).

My mother visited her regularly from Sussex Gardens. She had grown up believing her father to be William Waller, the postman who, a few years after her birth, moved in with Alice. Known to us as 'Willie', he was a dapper, well-read man who took a close interest in politics and edited the postmen's union journal. Alice was referred to as 'Mrs Waller', although it is possible they never married. Mother only discovered in 1960 that Willie was not her father when she came across her birth certificate in Alice's papers. Indeed, there was no father named at all. As her name was given as Waller on her passport, she had assumed her dad was Willie. Also amongst the papers was a court order dated July 1901, stating that Sir Alfred Burton, of Lincoln's Inn Fields, was to pay Alice Bond five shillings a week towards the upkeep of a female child until she reached the age of fourteen years. She assumed that Burton had been employed to handle the matter of maintenance by the wealthy family for whom Alice was working when she became pregnant. One of the families for whom Alice cooked on important occasions was the Sandemans, of the wine-importing fortune. It is likely they would have entertained Italian aristocrats. Mother believed it was significant that she was given the Italian name Elizina and was baptised into the Roman Catholic Church.

When Mother resigned from the WRNS in March 1919, she was still seeing her boyfriend George Burton, a young naval officer. They had promised to write to each other. She decided to go to London to seek work and gave him her mother's address – 33 Walton Street. Her mother told her she could stay no longer than a week. After a few days a letter arrived from George. Ella revealed the name of her suitor and her mother – as Ella would later describe – reacted like a mad woman. She snatched the letter, tore it up and threw the pieces on the fire, shouting that her daughter was too young for that sort of thing. The letter had been destroyed before Ella could take a note of George's new address. She was unable to reply and it was the end of the affair. Distraught, she ran from the house and bought a copy of *The Morning Post* that advertised vacant jobs. A bridge club in Knightsbridge needed a housemaid. It was run by two women – a Mrs Oakes and Lady Ward, wife of Sir Lesley Ward, the artist and cartoonist. Ward was particularly well known for his cartoons of public men, especially politicians, depicted with large heads and small bodies. Prints of them were displayed in clubs and restaurants all over London. Ella was interviewed by Lady Ward and started work the same day. A few weeks later the club steward asked her to help a teenage trainee waiter, Frederick Butler, my father-to-be.

When off-duty, Ella took him along to the Walton Street flat where he got on well with left-wing Willie. At heart, Fred was a natural Conservative who accepted what remained of the class system following the First World War. Soon, Frederick entered service as an under-footman with the Clifton-Brown family.

One of Willie's more important contacts was the Rev. Shepherd, Vicar of St Martin-in-the-Fields from 1914 to 1927. A popular leftist preacher and ardent pacifist, he was a clever propagandist and pioneered religious broadcasting. He worked hand-in-glove with left-wing pacifist politicians. Willie had regular meetings with him. Despite her Labour sympathies, my mother had challenged at least some of his opinions in debate with Willie and to win her over, he took her to meet Shepherd at his church in Trafalgar Square in 1928. The red vicar failed to convince her and to Willie's dismay, she later accused him of being a humbug and a hypocrite. Notwithstanding my mother's opinion, Shepherd was promoted to become Dean of Canterbury in 1929 and then Canon of St Paul's Cathedral in 1934.

Willie died in his sixties. An obituary written by one of his colleagues at the Post Office declared; 'Death has deprived us of another of the few remaining stalwarts of the great movement that fought against odds for the emancipation of his class... The Postmen's Federation.

'In the outer world, any project for the advancement of the workers found in Bill a fervent supporter. That he was the possessor of a broad mind, a big heart and a generous soul, many of his friends can testify.'

My mother, a young girl desperately in need of love and affection, saw nothing of Willie's big heart. To him she was a considerable nuisance. Coldly and cruelly, he made it clear that he did not want her around her mother's little flat.

During my last year at the LSE I was reintroduced to the teenage daughter of one of my mother's closest friends – Mary Luetchford. Mary, a girl from the West Coast of Ireland, had been a lady's maid at the house of the Sandeman family where my grandmother had cooked. She had married a chauffeur and motor mechanic Thomas Luetchford, from a leading family in Brighton. At six years old I had been presented to their six-week-old first and only child; a daughter, Evelyn.

I had seen her occasionally over the years and was impressed to learn she had won a scholarship to one of the finest girls' schools in Britain – the North London Collegiate. By 1951 she was in her final year there and I was asked to escort her to the school's annual ball. This was a smart, black-tie affair and I was pleased to do so, although soon after we arrived I was dumped for a younger model. At that age, the six years between us was quite significant. In time, it did not seem so great and I was to marry Evelyn in 1958. She soon fulfilled her ambition to become a fashion buyer at Harrods, the world-famous department store, and was the youngest they had ever had.

But before I was to set up home with Evelyn, as I prepared to head north in that summer of 1951, I received a letter from the War Office. Due to the threatening international situation, the government had decided to call up for two weeks' refresher training a category of ex-national servicemen – the 'Z Reservists'. The North Koreans had invaded South Korea the previous July, evidence that Communist regimes regarded war as an acceptable tactic to achieve their aims. The Attlee government had therefore decided to embark on an extensive rearmament programme, putting a strain on Britain's already weak economy. Despite the fact that our military strength was already severely stretched from holding a long line of defensive positions in the Middle East against the Communist threat, we were able, with the help of the USA, to send a brigade to Korea.

One of Britain's top soldiers involved in the high-level talks with the USA on how to combine against the growing international Communist threat was Marshal of the RAF, Lord Tedder, Chairman of the Joint Services Mission to Washington. My mother had known him well in the 1920s when, as an Air Force officer on the rise, he had married the rather dotty debutante daughter of Lina's closest friend, Lady Seton. Mother had helped on the wedding day.

My War Office letter told me to report to an ordnance vehicle depot at Tidworth in Gloucestersire, for which I was sent a travel warrant. I informed my new Kemsley Group employers, brushed the dust off my old Second Lieutenant's uniform and reported for duty. Thanks as ever to my father's skill with a pressing iron, I turned up in immaculate order. The Commanding Officer, a major, called up from running his own motor vehicle repair business, was somewhat crumpled. He eyed me with approval and asked me to take the roll-call parade in the morning. 'I'm afraid the men's kit appears to be in a bloody awful mess,' he remarked.

It was. If we were a typical Z Reserve unit then the man who encountered my mother on her way to sign up in the First World War might well exclaim once more; 'Gawd 'elp England!'

Faced with the threatening military might of the Soviet Army in Europe we were the equivalent of the 'forlorn hope' platoon of Wellington's army, assembled in a suicidal bid to achieve the virtually impossible in the face of overwhelming odds.

Apart from the reception for my smart turn-out, I received another plus. A senior regular army major arrived at the depot and immediately recognised me as someone with whom he had played rugby with the Ordnance Corps, four years earlier. He greeted me in the mess like a long-lost son. During the training I also had the luck to win a medal for best shot in the company – a feat the junior officer was expected to perform to win his men's respect.

But the high spot of the two weeks came at the weekend. Realising that Broadwell Farm was in easy reach I decided to call on Farmer Blanch and his wife Lilian, who had cared for me so well during my wartime evacuation in the Forest of Dean. In fact, their farm had become too much to manage and Milsom had sold it, moving on the proceeds to a modern house. There I found them, on an estate in nearby Berryhill, hardly changed in the ten years since I had seen them. We sat down to a lunch of juicy roast pork washed down with cider. Yes, it was so much better to have electric light and water that came from a tap instead of a deep well in the garden. Although I had written once in a while, they had never expected to see me again. That I had made the effort to visit delighted the old couple. The reunion was warm and wonderful for I was the nearest they had come to raising a son.

I should have left that memory as perfect. Instead I pushed my luck and long after Lil and Milsom had gone back to the earth they worked, in the autumn of 2011 Evelyn and I took a short holiday in the Forest of Dean. I decided to revisit the dear old farm. The village was hard to recognise. There had been a lot of rebuilding. A row of modern houses ran along the main road where Stephen Fowler's church hall had stood in which I trained to be a boy scout. Along the track that had led Alan Barton and me up to the farm that day in 1940, we reached a gate and I saw that the space that had been the farmyard was still there – as a car park – but the farmhouse and great barn were no more. In their place stood a modern house. Everything must change, but it saddened me and I regretted having returned.

At the end of my Z Reserve training the CO revealed that he had been asked to recruit for what was called the Army's Supplementary Reserve. Members were committed to two weeks training camp a year and attendance at an occasional lecture about the Soviet threat and the role of NATO. Unlike the Territorial Army, members could also be called up without a proclamation in time of emergency – such as the Suez fiasco. They were the front line reserve and received an annual bonus on top of the regular pay while in camp.

As I had enjoyed the training I promised to consider the offer, contingent on my being allowed the time off work. That permission was duly forthcoming from the Kemsley head office and I went on to serve for over twelve years in what was renamed the Army Emergency Reserve. In 1956, however, I found myself in an extremely invidious situation.

I had signed up assuming that should the Reserve actually be mobilised it would be to repel the Russkies. To my dismay Prime Minister Anthony Eden, a sick man whose once-sound judgement had gone to pieces, launched an illegal war against Egypt, a vulnerable Third World country, for having nationalised the Suez Canal Company – a valuable asset that could build national wealth. Eden's cynical plan, worthy of a fascist dictator, was to encourage Israel to invade Egypt and for the British and French forces to then support that attack should Egypt reject a ceasefire.

Eden and his pathetic Foreign Secretary, Selwyn Lloyd, both lied to Parliament, denying in the Commons that such a secret invasion plan existed. Members of the Army Emergency Reserve were called up to support the over-stretched regular army. So deeply opposed was I to the whole disgraceful plan that I decided to risk a court martial and refuse to be mobilised. The War Office must have decided discretion was the better part of objection and did not call on me.

Friends of mine who were summoned to serve found themselves in the midst of a military cock-up on a grand scale. In their book *Suez: The Double War*, Roy Fullick and Geoffrey Powell describe the chaos and confusion over the provision of vehicles that would have been my remit.

They vividly describe that when units such as mine went to collect vehicles they found many in a decrepit state and numerous items out of stock. The army had so few tank transporters that the removal firm Pickfords was asked to help. However, their workers were subject to trade union rules so that their transporters took a week to complete a journey that an army convoy could complete in three days. It took four weeks to move and load ninety-three tanks.

Confident that a Suez-style situation would not be repeated, I remained in the corps and was awarded the Emergency Reserve Decoration. Soon after that, however, I retired with the rank of captain. Frustrated by the on-going incompetence of the Whitehall warriors who kept us short of equipment and training, we remained the forlorn hope. The full scandal of the Defence Ministry's lack of preparedness and crippling inefficiency emerged when British troops were sent once more ill-equipped to the 2001 war in Afghanistan.

After the disappointment of my return to Broadwell Farm, I should perhaps have heeded E.M. Forster's edict; 'Never go back'. Yet in 2011 I found myself once more at the London School of Economics. Partly because the LSE had a well-deserved reputation for serving second-rate food in depressing surroundings I had avoided graduate reunions. Now I found myself enticed. As I entered Houghton Street I was faced by a throng of students filling the thoroughfare, scruffy, noisy and ill-mannered, many of them selling various journals and other stuff. One was even slumped by the curb, overcome by either drink or drugs.

Overshadowing the world-famous campus were two problems – firstly the school had slid down the league table of academic excellence and was no longer in the top three as it had been in my day. Secondly, it had damaged its proud record of independence by accepting a large sum of money from the Gaddafi International Charity and Development Foundation controlled by the notorious, since killed in the Arab democratic uprising, Libyan dictator Colonel Gaddafi. In return the LSE had admitted the Colonel's vicious son Saif in 2002 and allowed him to be awarded a Ph.D. in Philosophy, despite the concerns voiced about his academic ability.

The LSE's links with the appalling Libyan regime – in tune with Tony Blair's government of the time – became so strong it was nicknamed the 'Libyan School of Economics'. As the scandal unfolded, the disgraced LSE Director Sir Howard Davies resigned. It was recalled that when the governing council of the LSE discussed whether to accept a donation of £1.5 million from Saif Gaddafi, the school's Professor of International Relations Fred Halliday warned the money would taint the university's reputation. I hope my dear friend Martin Wight would have been proud of his stand. Still, it was deemed more important not to cause personal embarrassment to the odious Saif and so the dirty loot was accepted (of which £300,000 was subsequently paid).

Despite damage to its reputation by the Libyan scandal and its failure to maintain its once high academic standards, the LSE did well in *The Times* newspaper's *Good University Guide* for the academic year September 2013. It was rated third after Oxford and Cambridge in such areas as student satisfaction, research quality and graduate prospects.

More important to me than the state of the institution was my continued friendship with five people who studied alongside me in the International Relations Department over sixty years ago. As there were only about twenty members in the 1948 intake it seems extraordinary that six of us, all over eighty, have remained in touch into 2012. They include Sir David Elliot and Ronald Brandon, who accompanied me on the hitchhike around Europe. The others were John Lester, Ian Ogilvie and Neville Beale. Maybe studying International Relations is a key to longevity?

Sadly, Neville, a leading figure in London Tory Party circles for years, left our exclusive club in March 2012, having reached the fine age of eighty-six. A few days after he died I discovered a note he had sent with a clipping of a letter he had had published in *The Spectator* early in 1999. It concerned his one-time contact, the famous Russian KGB defector Oleg Gordievsky. Neville recalled that during his three years in London, ostensibly as a diplomat, Gordievsky had lunch with him every few months in some of the best restaurants. He wrote; 'My only importance to him (and his superiors?) seems to have been my apparent closeness – as the Member for Finchley on the Greater London Council – to the Prime Minister who represented the same constituency in the House of Commons, Mrs Thatcher. The only thing he ever asked about her, however, was the state of her health, which I easily described as robust.'

In due course, Neville helped to save Gordievsky's life. The Russian double agent cancelled their next lunch because, to his surprise, he had been recalled early to Moscow, where he was put in a 'sanatorium'. Neville alerted his British contacts and a rescue operation spirited him out of the Soviet Union.

After defecting, Gordievsky – who had been acting head of Soviet intelligence in London – produced lists for MI5 of British politicians, trade union figures and journalists who had been regarded as useful contacts by the KGB. They were wrongly described in reports to the Kremlin as having been persuaded to support the Moscow line. Around the same time, MI5 wasted time, I believe, by having my house burgled. Having discovered nothing they called me in for a 'chat' (events detailed in my first volume of memoirs, *People, Politics and Pressure Groups*). Gordievsky, or some other defector, had revealed that, as a political and diplomatic correspondent for national newspapers for over a dozen years, I had held regular lunchtime meetings with Soviet bloc spies.

My first Russian spy contact, in fact, was the shrewdly successful KGB colonel Mikhail Lyubimov, who from his retirement wrote a letter to *The Times* in February 1995. In it, he accused Gordievsky of telling half-truths and being caught up in a KGB rat race that had little connection with reality.

At Neville's funeral, his partner Rosemary told me that she had found Gordievsky's phone number in his contacts book. She called him and relayed that he sounded sad when told of his death. At about the same time, the famous old defector burst into the press again. He had a warning that the number of Russian spies in Britain could be greater than in the mid-1980s when thirty-nine intelligence officers were based in the London embassy. The *Daily Telegraph* reported on 7 April 2012 that there were fears that Russia, ruled by the macho Putin, would intensify its operations over coming months while Britain's over-stretched services had to focus on the Queen's Diamond Jubilee and the Olympic Games.

I was glad to be professionally clear of the murky world of spooks and spies but that episode only added to the interest of my life. I was one of that fortunate generation just young enough to miss being called upon to serve in the Second World War, yet old enough to benefit from the short-lived but monumental improvement in education introduced by R.A.

Butler and the Welfare State designed by William Beveridge – under the guidance of our remarkable wartime coalition government.

Thanks to these advantages, that neither my grandmother Alice nor my parents could have foreseen as possible, I was able to prosper and progress, living a fulfilling and comfortable life. I attended one of the finest educational institutions in the world; served as a peacetime army officer; achieved my ambition to work in Parliament as a national newspaper journalist; and concluded my career as a parliamentary adviser to some of the great organisations in the world, General Motors and the Corporation of the City of London amongst them. On reflection, I should hardly complain that I never got to India.

Epilogue:
Mail from the Front Line

My grandmother Alice's beloved brother Private Alfred Bond fought in some of the fiercest encounters of the Boer War – what has been called the last of the Gentlemen's Wars. Sandwiched between the Crimean and the First World War, it was the war in which the famous scarlet tunic and white cross belts of the British infantry gave place to drab khaki, making it more difficult for the expert Boer marksmen, armed with Mauser rifles, to hit their target.

Alfred's letters reveal that he was involved in the ill-conceived and costly attack on the Boer stronghold of Colenso – one of the five major battles of the war. Under the command of the brave but incompetent General Sir Redvers Buller VC, it was, according to *The Times. History of the Boer War*, 'a frontal attack directed on three points of an insufficiently reconnoitered position held in unknown strength by an entrenched enemy… A worse plan could not have been devised.' It was, in short, a disaster.

The following letter from Alfred describes an engagement in the run-up to Colenso:

8 Dec 1899
Dear Alice,
I expect you read in the papers about the battle. Our regiment had no joke. It was a bit tight to see the wounded. I had the job to carry some as the stretcher-bearers could

not get up in the firing line. One chap had a wound in his leg and he died through loss of blood. Of course, we had several killed beside him but we did not half make the Boers run. We captured horses and a lot of meat and treacle and several other things. But we had to retire as the day went on as we were fairly outnumbered – 7000 Boers against 2000 of us. But we killed such a lot of them I got the cramp looking at them. Well Alice, they are a dirty looking lot, dressed like a lot of tramps.

When we charged up the hill at them at daybreak one of them shouted 'Halt, who goes there' (he was an Englishman – they have a lot of English fighting for them) and before he had time to get an answer he had about ten of our bayonets sticking through his ribs. He gave a couple of groans, handed over his dinner and fell back dead. I went down his pockets to see if he had any money but he did not have any. Well Alice, we were firing at each other all day and I found myself behind a big rock – about the size of The Latchmere [a famous public house in Battersea] – with bullets and shells flying around us. Well Alice, it is a fact, while they were firing we were advancing up to them, singing for old times sake.

I am on outpost duty with my company. Things are a bit rough here. If you could get a box of Woodbine fags and send them to me I would be very pleased.

More letters followed:

1 January 1900
My dear Alice,
Very pleased to receive your kind and welcome letter ... I have seen Charlie twice. He seemed happy enough and for good reason. He doesn't do any fighting and is shoeing

mules and donkeys all the time… We have had another couple of fights and you would laugh to see us ducking our heads when the Boers start shelling us. It is a bit tight to see all our killed and wounded being carried away. We don't know how many of the Boers we kill as they take them away.

The grub we get is a bit thick, so if you have got a couple of spare bones to give away you might think of me.

Did you see in the papers about one of our officers being shot? Well, he had just taken myself and another chap around a hill and was taking two more around when he and one of the others got killed. So you see, I had a very narrow escape.

We are getting a lot of our wounded back. If they get shot through the arm or the leg without the bullet touching the bone it takes only about three weeks or a month to get better again…

We have only just been back in camp a couple of days after having a good day's fighting, with no tents and soaking wet through, and it is terribly cold at nights…

Don't forget the fags.

* * *

11 February, 1900
Dear Alice,
Many thanks for your letter and box of fags which I received yesterday. We were on the march from Spearmans Hill back to Colenso when I got it. All my chums gathered round to see what was in the parcel and when we saw fags every hair in my head stood up with excitement.

Well Alice old girl, we are having it a bit thick again … especially in our last eight days fighting. On one day we had the most shelling I have seen and it is a wonder I am left to tell the tale. One shell burst right among our post, killing one chap. It broke our Captain's arm and two ribs and busted his head. I was sitting on the top of a hill we had taken when a shell came over very close. I could hear it coming and it burst just over our heads, the back part falling right through a waterproof sheet that was keeping the sun off me. It fell just between my feet – so you see my day had not yet come.

But it is a treat to see some of the cowards tremble. They say English soldiers have no fear – but if they were out here they would see a few proper big cowards frightened to move. They do make one wild when one is trying to do his best.

Well Alice, we have shifted back to Colenso, the place where we had so many killed and wounded and we believe we are going to try another attack in a day or so. I am looking forward to coming out all right. I am rather lucky. I have seen as much fighting out here as most and I have not been hit yet. But I must not brag about it as there is a lot more to go through...

There certainly was. But Alfred would not be taken out by a bullet or shell at Colenso. Like so many others in that South African Field Force, he perished from the dreaded dysentery. As for General Buller, he was removed from supreme command.

Bibliography

Abse, Joan (editor) – *My LSE*, Robson Books, 1977.

Bradley Hill Workshop – *The Royal Forest of Dean*, 1988.

Blunden, Edmund – *Shelley*, Collins, 1946.

Chambers, Harris and Bayley – *This Age of Conflict*, Harcourt, Brace & Co., 1950.

De Chirico, Giorgio – *The Memoirs*, Peter Owen Ltd., 1971.

Forster, E.M. – *A Passage to India*, Penguin, 1943.

Fitzgerald, F. Scott – *The Great Gatsby*, Chatto & Windus, 1926.

Gardner, Helen – *The New Oxford Book of English Verse*, Book Club Associates, 1984.

Greenslade, Roy – *Press Gang*, Macmillan, 2003.

Hampton, Janice – *Austerity Olympics*, Aurum Press, 2012.

Harris, Rex – *Jazz*, Pelican, 1952.

Haskell, Arnold – *Ballet*, Pelican, 1949.

Hastings, Max – *Armageddon*, Pan Books, 2005.

Jones, Alan – *An Enchanted Journey*, Pentland Press, 1994.

Leasor, James – *The Sergeant-Major*, George Harrap & Co., 1955.

MacCarthy, Desmond – *Humanities*, McGibbon & Kee, 1953.

Machiavelli, Nicolo – *The Prince*, Penguin Classics, 1990.

Morgenthau and Thompson – *Principles & Problems of International Politics*, Knopf, 1950.

Pemberton, W. Baring – *Battles of the Boer War*, Pan Books, 1972.

Powell, David – *The Power Game*, Duckworth, 1993.

Fullick, Roy and Powell, Geoffrey – *Suez: The Double War*, Hamish Hamilton, 1979.

Thucydides – *The Peloponnesian War*, Everyman, 1948.

Wight, Martin – *Power Politics*, Pelican Books, 1979.

Williams, Francis – *A Prime Minister Remembers*, Heinemann, 1961.

Yeats, W.B. – *Collected Poems*, Macmillan, 1950.

Index

18th (Prince of Wales' own) Tiwana
    Lancers 2
33 Walton Street 22, 132
    see also Walton Street
49 Grosvenor Square 34
    see also Grosvenor Square
64 Richmond Street 9, 10, 11
145 Piccadilly 1, 30
506th Parachute Infantry Regiment
    60

Admiralty 104
Afghanistan 138
Africa 55, 59, 101, 131
    see also Boer War
Aga Khan 17, 18
Agnes 5–6
Albany, Piccadilly 24
Aldbourne 60
Aldershot 81
Alford, Jim 61
Alfred (brother of Alice) 8
    see also Bond, Private Alfred
Alfred (cousin of Ella) 12, 28
Alice (cousin of Ella) 12
Alice (grandmother of Arthur) 2,
    4–9, 12, 13, 33–4, 102
    arranging piano lessons 66–7
    attitude to daughter 10, 15,
        16–17, 20, 22, 38

and ballet 109
and brother 143–6
in Clock Tower apartment 48, 49
and father of Ella 132
record collection 36
at Selfridges 49–50
and William Waller 131–2
working for Lina 3
Aly Khan, Prince 17–18
Ames, Captain Oswald 7
Angel Face 41
Annan, Noel 98
Anouilh, Jean 128
The Apostles 103
Appointments' Board,
    Universities 126, 127
Appollinaire, Guillaume 110
Armageddon (Hastings) 60
Arms and the Man (Shaw) 102
Armstrong, Louis 'Satchmo' 26, 67
Army Emergency Reserve 137–8
Army's Supplementary Reserve 137
Art Society, LSE 104, 108, 109,
    111, 113
Ashworth, Jon 23
Astaire, Fred 33
Atlantic Hotel, Hamburg 92
Attlee, Clem 62, 63, 77, 81–2, 98,
    124, 129
Auden, Michael 73

Auden, W.H. 73
Austria 66
Auxiliary Fire Service 40

Babette's Feast 7–8
Baden-Powell, Lady 48–9
Bailey, Captain 80
Baird, John Logie 73
Baker, Kenny 68
Baldwin, Stanley 30, 35
Ballet (Haskell) 108
Baltic coast 93, 94
Band of Brothers 60
Bargello Fortress 118
Barton, Alan 42–3, 45, 47, 51, 52,
    53, 55, 61, 130
Barton-Chapple, Derek (later
    Waring) 73, 81, 84
Barton-Chapple, Wing Commander
    Harry 73
Bavaria 95
Bayley, Charles 101
Beadle, David 120
Beale, Neville 140, 141
Beaverbrook, Lord 28, 126
Beethoven, Ludwig van 92
Bell, Clive 103
Bell's Grammar School 47
Bell, Vanessa 103
Bengal Lancers 2, 7
Berlin 94
Berlin Airlift 96
Berlin games 97
Bermant, Chaim 99
Bern 116–17
Berry, Gomer (later Lord
    Kemsley) 127
Berryhill 55, 136
Bertie, Prince of Wales (later King
    Edward VII) 6
Bevan, Nye 125, 127, 129
Beveridge, William 98, 142
Biennale 110, 117–18
Bishops Stortford 79

Blair Government 139
Blanch, Lillian 45, 46, 51, 52, 53,
    55, 136
Blanch, Milson 45, 52, 55, 136
Blankers-Koen, Fanny 97
Blimp, Colonel 28
Blixen, Karen 7–8
Bloomsbury Group 103
Blossom 12
    see also Alice (grandmother of
        Arthur)
Blunden, Edmund 118–19
Boer War 8, 15, 131, 143–6
Bond, Alice 132
    see also Alice (grandmother of
        Arthur)
Bond, Private Alfred 143–6
    see also Alfred (brother of Alice)
Bonn 116
Bonn University 114, 116
Boulevard de Clichy 115
Boulevard St Germain 121
Boy Scout troop 51
Bradford, Countess of 2
Brandon, Ronald 114, 117, 118,
    119, 140
Brigade of Guards 69
British Army of the Rhine
    (BAOR) 87–96, 127
British Control Commission 93
British Embassy, Washington 20
British Empire 41–2
British Government 96, 97
Brittain, RSM Ronald 83
Britten, Benjamin 88
Broadwell Church 129
Broadwell Farm 43, 45–6, 51–4, 67,
    136–7
Brompton Road 131
Brown, Chris 14, 28
Browning, Robert 63
Brown Shipley Bank 22, 23, 27, 29
Bryanston Court 3
Buckingham Palace 1, 2

Buller, General Sir Redvers VC 143, 146
Burton, George 132
Burton Professor of International Relations 99
Burton, Sir Alfred 9, 132
Butler, Arthur
  childhood 25–6, 28–9, 30–1, 32–8, 39–43, 45–7, 48, 49, 51–68
  at LSE 98–107, 108–11, 112–13, 123–4, 125–6, 127–8
  national service 68–70, 72–81, 82–96
Butler, Caroline 79
Butler Education Act 65–6
Butler, Evelyn (née Luetchford) 136
  see also Luetchford, Evelyn (later Butler)
Butler, Frederick 28, 31, 32, 49, 76, 113–14
  employment 22, 27, 29
  and gambling 33
  meeting Ella 21, 133
  in the Second World War 40, 42, 48, 51, 54, 55–6, 59, 66
  travels 130
Butler, grandparents of Arthur 32, 58–9
Butler, Richard Austen 'Rab' 65, 66, 141–2

Café Flore 121
Cairncross, Alec 63
Calcutta 71
Cambridge University 79, 102, 139
Camrose, Lord 127
Camus, Albert 121
Cannes 120
Canterbury, Dean 133
Carrie 9
Carr-Saunders, Sir Alexander 110, 111
Caruso, Enrico 19

Caterham 69, 72, 73, 74–6, 77–81
Chamberlain, Neville 39–40, 42
Chambers, Frank 101
Chaplin, Charlie 53
Charles Street, Mayfair 107
Charlie 12, 14
Charter Cup essay prize 76
Chartier restaurant 115, 120
Chatham House 123
Chelsea 25–6, 49
  see also Walton Street
Chelsea Town Hall 26
Chess Club, LSE 104, 106
Chingford County High School 42–3
Christian Dior, House of 122
Churchill, Winston 40, 62, 63, 92, 124
CIA 107
City of London 51
City of London Corporation 142
Civil Service 128
Clarke, Brigadier Terence 86
Clifton-Brown, Colonel 22
Clifton-Brown family 21, 133
Clock Tower, Hampton Court Palace 48–9, 102
Coalition Government 97
Cockhouse captain's efficiency prize 76
Cold War 96
Coleford, Gloucestershire 42–3, 45–8, 51
Colenso 143, 145, 146
Cologne 116
Como, Lake 117
Congress Party 71, 72
Conservative Party 62, 78, 124, 125
Cooks Ferry Inn 68
Coolidge, President 20
Cooper, Gary 33
Cooper, James Fenimore 48
Copeman, John 107
Coppet Hill 52

Corporation of the City of London 142
Coryate, Thomas 117
Courtauld, Samuel 66
Courtauld, Sydney Elizabeth 66
Crawford, Marion ('Crawfie') 1
Crillon Hotel 18, 130
Cripps, Sir Stafford 124, 128–9
La Croisette 120
Crystal Palace 31
Cunard, Lady 3
Czechoslovakia 39, 89, 96

Daily Express 28
Daily Herald 28
The Daily Sketch 127
Daily Telegraph 108, 141
'Dai the Milk' 25–6
Dali, Salvador 26, 110
Dalton, Hugh 60, 87, 98
Dansie, Colonel Bill 91
David (Edward, Prince of Wales, later Edward VIII, then Duke of Windsor) 2, 3, 30, 35
David, statue 118
Davies, Sir Howard 139
Davis, Henry William Bank 36
de Beauvoir, Simone 121
de Chirico, Giorgio 109–11
Defence Ministry 138
Delhi Durbar 34
Desert Air Force 55
de Valois, Ninette 109
de Waal, Edmund 73
Diaghilev, Sergei 108
Dior, Christian 122
Diplomatic Corps 128
Donatello 118
Don Juan (yacht) 119
Doodlebug 57–8
Dookie 1
Dover 11–15, 16, 26–7
Doxford, Mrs 51, 90
Drill Factory 69, 73

Dulwich Picture Gallery 111–12, 113
Dyer, Major Thistleton 74, 80
Dying Swan 109
Dyson, Geoffrey 61

Eastern Avenue 38
Easy Company of the 506th Parachute Infantry Regiment 60
Economic Consequences of the Peace (Keynes) 102
The Economist 102
Eden, Anthony 137
Edgware Road 9
Edmonton 68
Edward, Prince of Wales (David, later Edward VIII, then Duke of Windsor) 2, 3, 30, 35
Edward VII, King 6, 11
Egypt 137
'Eleven Plus' examination 40
Elizabeth II, Queen 7
Elizabeth, Princess (later Elizabeth II) 1, 2, 35, 86
Ella (Elizina) 9–13, 16–21, 22–3, 26–8, 32, 107, 113–14, 130
  arranging piano lessons 66–7
  and ballet 109
  boyfriends 132–3
  childhood 9–13
  falling into the Serpentine 35
  on fashion 121
  in the First World War 14–15
  liking for films 33
  and Lord Tedder 135
  relationship with Willie Waller 134
  in the Second World War 40, 42, 51, 55, 56–7
  at Selfridges 49, 50–1
  and the theatre 128
  travels 36, 37, 119, 130
  visits to mother 34, 131
  see also mother of Arthur Butler

Elliott, Geoffrey 61, 96
Elliot, David (later Sir) 114, 117, 140
Emergency Reserve Decoration 138
English-Speaking Union (ESU) 106–7, 108
Essex 37–9, 40–1, 48, 54, 55, 59, 67
Eugénie, Empress 15–16, 121
European Community 92
Evening Gazette, Middlesbrough 127
Evening Standard 28
Exeter University 130
Exhibition of Metaphysical Painting 110
Fabian Society 126
Fairholme Avenue, Gidea Park 37–8, 39
Farnborough Hill 15
father of Arthur Butler *see* Butler, Frederick
Faversham, Kent 27
Feltham, Middlesex 84–5
Fire Service, Auxiliary 40
First World War 14–15, 16
Fisher, Lady 48
Fitzgerald, F. Scott 21
Fleet Street 126
Florence (city) 118
Florrie 16
Foot, Michael 78
Foreign Office 47, 128
Forest of Dean 46–7, 136
Forggensee Lake 95
Forster, E.M. 70
Four Seasons Hotel, Hamburg 91
Fowler, Rev. Stephen 51, 53, 129–30
France 17, 18, 19, 20, 114–16, 119–20
Franco, General 39
Fraser, James 127
Freeman, John 129
Fry, Christopher 128

Fry, Roger 102
Fullick, Roy 138
Furness, Lord 3–4
Furness, Viscountess Thelma 3

Gaddafi, Colonel 139
Gaddafi International Charity and Development Foundation 139
Gaddafi, Saif 139
Gaitskell, Hugh 77, 129
Garmisch 95
Garrick, David 102
Garrick's Villa, Hampton 102, 125–6
The Gay Divorcee 33
General Motors 142
George (cousin) 12, 28, 39
George VI, King 2, 32
George V, King 1–2, 11, 31
Georgian Group 113
Germany 38, 39, 87–96, 97, 114, 116
Gidea Park 37–8, 39, 48, 67
Gielgud, John 108
Giles 131
Gladstone Memorial Essay prize 125
Gladstone, William 125
Gloucestershire 42–3, 45–8, 51–5, 135–7
Godson, Joe 107–8
Good University Guide 139
Gordievsky, Oleg 140–1
grandparents of Arthur Butler *see* Alice (grandmother of Arthur); Butler, grandparents of Arthur
Grant, Duncan 103
The Graphic 127
The Great Dictator 53
Greece 96
Green Park 1
Grey, Earl, Governor General of Canada 2
Grill Room, Savoy Hotel 24
Grosvenor Square 2, 3, 34

Guards Depot 69, 73–80
Guernica 39
Gurkha regiments 72
Guy's Hospital, London 95

Halliday, Fred 139
Hamburg 91–3
Hampton 102
Hampton Court Palace 48–9, 102
Hans 90, 91–2, 93, 94
The Hare with Amber Eyes (de
    Waal) 73
Harris, Air Marshal 'Bomber' 92
Harris, Christina Phelps 101
Harrods 134
Haskell, Arnold 108–9
Hastings, Max 60
Hastings Wood House 54, 55
Haute Ecole Commercial 114
Hayworth, Rita 18
Healey, Denis 47, 107
Heath, Sir Edward 23–4
Heath, Ted (band) 68
Heaven, Sidney 61
Henty, G.A. 41
Hepworth, Barbara 118
Higher School Certificate 61, 76
Hitler, Adolf 33, 53, 54
Hobson, Harold 128
Holland 87, 97
Holst, Gustav 65, 79
'Honky-Tonk Train Blues' 67
Horne, Lena 130
Houghton Street 98–9, 138–9
    see also London School of
        Economics (LSE)
House of Commons 23–4
House of Worth 121
Hyde Park 35, 131

I am a Camera (Isherwood) 73
If (Kipling) 36
Ile Sainte-Marguerite 120
Imperial Tobacco Company 47

India 71–2, 81–2
Indian Army 33, 34, 68–9, 72,
    74–6, 85, 90
Intelligence Corps 79
inter-BSc (Economics) 72, 76, 92, 93
International Relations Department,
    LSE 99–100, 114, 123–4, 140
Introduction to Economics
    (Cairncross) 63
L'Invitation au Chateau (Anouilh,
    trans. Fry) 128
Isherwood, Christopher 73
Israel 96–7, 137
Italian countess 8–9
Italy 18–19, 38, 39, 59

Jacobs, Ida 70
James Allen's Girls', Dulwich 79
Jane 5–6
Japan 97
Jinnah, Mr 71
Joseph, A.F. 40

Karen 93, 94, 96
Karim, Prince 18
Keats, John 119
Kemsley Editorial Training Plan 126,
    130
Kemsley, Lord (born Gomer
    Berry) 126, 127
Kemsley Newspapers group 126,
    127, 135, 137
Kent 27
Keynes, John Maynard 102–3
KGB 141
Khan, Prince Aly 37
'King of Sind' 85
Kipling, Rudyard 36
Klagenfurt 66
Knightsbridge 21
Knightsbridge Green 4
Knott, Barbara 112, 113
Korea 123, 134, 135
Kremlin 141

Labour Congress 1917 104
Labour Government 71, 78, 87, 98, 124, 129, 134–5
Labour Party 21–2, 29, 62–3, 107, 125, 128–9
Labour Society, LSE 104, 105–6
The Lady's Not For Burning (Fry) 128
Lamb, Henry 102
Laski, Professor Harold 98, 100
The Last of the Mohicans (James Fenimore Cooper) 48
Le Bond, Charles 4
Lehar, Franz 88
Leigh-Mallory, Air Chief Marshall 55
Lerici 118–19, 120
Lester, John 140
Levin, Bernard 104, 105–6
Lewis, Meade Lux 67
Leyton Labour Party 125
Leytonstone 56, 67, 130–1
Leytonstone Express and Independent 59
Libya 139
Lido nightclub 115
Limelight 53
Lina (Caroline Sinnickson, later Caroline Offley Shore) 2–3, 22, 32, 101–2, 135
  death 131
  and ESU 106–7
  and fashion 121, 122
  grace and favour apartment 48, 49
  and lead soldiers 34
  offering Ella a job 16–17
  travels 18–21, 37, 119, 130
Lindbergh, Charles 20
Lives of a Bengal Lancer 33, 68
Lloyd, Selwyn 137
London School of Economics (LSE) 47, 85, 90, 98–101, 129, 134, 138–40
  Chess Club 104
  exams 127–8
  Martin Wight 123–4
London University 76

see also London School of Economics (LSE)
The Long Afternoon (Waterfield) 119
Lothian, Lord 20
Lough, Ernest 36
Louvre 120
Low, David 28
Ludwig, King 95
Luetchford, Evelyn (later Butler) 134
see also Butler, Evelyn (née Luetchford)
Luetchford, Mary 134
Luetchford, Thomas 3, 134
Luftwaffe 42
Lugarno 117
Lyttleton, Humphrey 68
Lyubimov, Mikhail 141

MacCarthy, Desmond 102, 103–4, 125–6, 127, 130
MacCarthy, Mary 102, 125, 130
MacDonald, Ramsay 29
Machiavelli, Niccolò 119
Maclean-Harris, Isobel 107
Macmillan, Harold 47
Major, John 97
Manning, Professor Charles 99, 101
Margaret, Princess 1, 2, 35
Markova, Alicia 108
Marlborough Buildings 25–6
Marlborough School 26
Marshall, Harvey 105–6
Mary, Princess (later Queen Mary) 2
Mary, Queen 31–2
Maxwell, Robert 48
May (cousin of Ella) 12
Mayfair 107
Mellon, Paul 111–12
Menton 119–20
The Merry Widow (Lehar) 88
Metaphysical Painting, Exhibition of 110
MI5 30, 53, 140–1

Michelangelo 118
Middle East 68, 96–7, 135, 137
Middlesbrough 130
Middlesbrough *Evening Gazette* 127
Mighty Joe Young 118
Miners' Federation 29
Molyneux, Captain Edward
    MC 121, 122
Mona Lisa 120
Monmouth 52
Monro, David 120
Mons Barracks 81, 82–4
Monte Carlo 119, 120
Morgan, John 47–8, 128
Morgenthau, Professor Hans 124
The Morning Post 132
Morris, Alf, Lord Morris of
    Manchester 105
Morrison, Herbert 58
Morrow, Anne 20
Mother and Son (Henry William
    Bank Davis) 36
mother of Arthur Butler 1, 3
    see also Ella (Elizina)
Mountbatten, Earl 81
Muslim League 71, 72
Mussolini, Benito 38, 63–4
Mutton Lancers 74
My Last Duchess (Browning) 63
My LSE 99

Naples 19
Napoleon III 15
National Executive Committee 125
National Gallery of Art,
    Washington 112
National Health Service 129
NATO 108
Naval Intelligence 104
Nazis 38, 39, 42
Nehru, Pandit 71
Nell (aunt) 11, 12–13, 14, 15,
    28–9, 30, 67
Nell (kitchen maid) 5–6

Netherlands 87, 97
Neuschwanstein Castle 95
New Statesman (NS) 102, 126
New York 20, 26
Nice 19
Nicholls, Major 'Bum' 69
Ninth Symphony (Beethoven) 92
Norderney 88
Norman, Montagu 23
North Africa 55, 59
Northfields 51
North Korea 123, 134
North London Collegiate 134
North Weald Aerodrome 54, 55
Nuffield College, Oxford 123

Oakeshott, Professor Michael 100
Oakes, Mrs 132
Oberammergau 95
The Observer 123, 126
Ode to Joy (Schiller) 92
Officer Cadet Training Unit
    (OCTU) 81
Offley Shore, Caroline *see* Lina
    (Caroline Sinnickson, later
    Caroline Offley Shore)
Offley Shore, Colonel Bohun Stovin
    Fairless 2, 17, 32, 34
'O for the Wings of a Dove' 36
Ogilvie, Ian 140
Oldenburg 87–91, 95–6
Oliver, Joe 'King' 67
Olympic Games 61, 96–7
Ordnance Corps 81, 82–96, 136
Ordnance Regimental Depot 49
Oxford University 78, 123, 139

Pakistan 81
Palace of Westminster 31
Palestine police 68
Pardoe, Geoffrey 62
Paris 20, 114–16, 120–2, 130
Paris Cinema 68
Parkes, John 95

Park Lane 32
Parlophone 67
Parnell, Jack 68
A Passage to India (Forster) 70
Passion Play (Oberammergau) 95
Pavlova, Anna 109
The Peloponnesian War
    (Thucydides) 119
PEN club 130
Pennies from Heaven 26
People, Politics and Pressure Groups
    (Butler) 141
Peter Grimes (Britten) 88
Philadelphia 19
Philip, Prince 86
Piccadilly 1, 2, 24, 30
Pickfords 138
Pigalle 114–15
Pike, Wing Commander Thomas
    (later Air Chief Marshal, Sir) 51,
    54, 55–6, 59
Pitman's Commercial College 100
Place de la Concorde 120
Place de St Germain 121
Poland 42
Pompeii Exhibition 47
Porter, Cole 33
Powell, Geoffrey 138
Power Politics (Wight) 124
Press Council 126
Prince Imperial 15
The Prince (Machiavelli) 119
Putterill, Reverend 'Red' Jack 65

Queens, New York 26
Queen's Royal Regiment 74

RAF 48, 51, 54, 130
Randall, Freddy 68
The Rape of the Sabine Women 49
Rawlings, George 12, 14
Red 93, 94
Red Cross 103
Republican Popular Front 38–9

Richmond Street 9, 10, 11
Ring Round the Moon (Fry) 128
Rittenhouse Square 19
Robbins, Lionel 100
Rococo Linderhof 95
Rogers, Ginger 33
Rome 118
Root, Alan 78–9
Root, Mrs 79
Rosemary 141
Rosengarten, Emma (later
    Sinnickson) 17
Rosengarten, George 17
Rose Rouge 120
Rosie 14
Royal Academy of Art 47, 111
Royal Army Ordnance Corps 81,
    82–96, 136
Royal Asiatic Society 113
Royal Ballet School 109
Royal Commission on the Press 126
Royal Court Theatre 131
Royal Naval Volunteer Reserve 104
Royal Society of British Artists 109
Rue Royale 122
Russell, Bertrand 103
Russia 94–5, 141
    see also Soviet Union

Sadler's Wells Ballet School 108–9
Salisbury Road Elementary 40–1
Sandeman family 132, 134
Sandhurst 76
San Remo 119
Sartre, Jean-Paul 121
Savoy Hotel 24
Schiller, Friedrich von 92
Schlesinger, Arthur 124
Scotland 31
Second of Foot 74
Second World War 42–62
Selfridge, Harry 50–1
Selfridges 8, 49–50
La Serenissima 118

Serpentine 35, 131
Seton, Lady 135
Shakespeare 131
Shannon, Earl 32
Sharp, Clifford 126
Shaw, George Bernard 102, 126
Shelley, Percy Bysshe 118–19
Shepherd, Rev. 133
Shinwell, Emmanuel ('Manny') 77
Shore, Caroline Offley *see* Lina
     (Caroline Sinnickson, later
     Caroline Offley Shore)
Shore, Colonel Offley Bohun Stovin
     Fairless 2, 17, 32, 34
Simpson, Mrs Wallis 2–3, 30
Sinnickson, Caroline (Lina, later
     Caroline Offley Shore) *see* Lina
     (Caroline Sinnickson, later
     Caroline Offley Shore)
Sinnickson, Charles 17
Sinnickson, Emma (née
     Rosengarten) 17
Sloane Square 131
Snap Farm 59–60
Soane, Sir John 112, 113
Sorensen, Rev. Reginald 56, 63, 125
South Africa 101, 131
     see also Boer War
South Korea 134
Soviet Union 96
     see also Russia
Spain 38–9
Spearmans Hill 145
The Spectator 140
Stanford University Business School 79
St Anne's Convent, Soho 8
St Germain 121
St Giles' churchyard 51
St Martin-in-the-Fields, Vicar 133
Stonehouse, John 104–5, 106
St Paul's Cathedral, Canon 133
Strachey, John 63, 87
Strachey, Lytton 103
St Saviours 36

Suez Canal Company 137
Suez: The Double War (Fullick and
     Powell) 138
Sullivan, Sir Arthur 6
Summerson, John 113
Sunday Express 131
The Sunday Times 102, 128
Sussex Gardens 130, 131
Switzerland 116–17
Symonds Yat 52

Tallon, William 31
Tangmere RAF station 51, 54
Tauber, Richard 36
Tawney, R.H. 98
Tedder, Lord 135
Thaxted 65
Thelma, Viscountess Furness 3
This Age of Conflict (Chambers et
     al.) 101
Thorpe, Jeremy 107
Thucydides 119
Tidworth 84, 135–7
The Times 27, 61, 139, 141
*The Times History of the Boer
     War* 143
Tito 90
Tiwana Lancers 2
Tone, Franchot 33
Top Hat 33
Tories 62, 78, 124, 125
La Tour d'Argent 121
Trade Union Movement 107–8
Travemünde 93, 94
Trevelyan, G.M. 103
Trinity College, Cambridge 103
Tuffin, Mrs 9, 10–11, 12
Tuileries 120
Tutin, Dorothy 73

Uffizi Gallery 118
Umberto, King 118
The Uncertainty of the Poet (de
     Chirico) 110

Universities Appointments
    Board 126, 127
University of Bonn 114, 116
USA 108, 135
    army 60
    State Department 107

V–1 flying bomb 57–8
V–2s 58
Vanderbilt, Gloria 19
Venice 117–18
Venice Biennale, 1948 110, 117–18
Venus Observed (Fry) 128
Vesuvius 36–7
Viceroy's Council 71
Victoria, Queen 6–7

Waddup, Graham 41
Wagner, Richard 95
Wales, Prince of, Bertie (later King
    Edward VII) 6
    see also Edward VII, King
Wales, Prince of (Edward, known as
    David) 2, 3, 30, 35
Waller, Alice *see* Alice (grandmother
    of Arthur)
Waller, William (Willie) 15, 22,
    131, 132, 133–4
Walthamstow dog track 66
Walton Street 22, 25, 48, 131
Wanstead Flats 59
Wanstead High School 40, 42, 48,
    54, 59–62, 69–70
    prize giving 76
    training athletes 96, 97–8
    V–2 bombing 58
Ward, Lady 132, 133
Ward, Sir Lesley 132–3
Waring, Richard 73
Warley Woods 38
War Office 134, 135, 138
War Office Selection Board
    (WOSB) 69, 80

Washington 20
Waterfield, Giles 111–12, 119
Waugh, Auberon 69
Wavell, Lord 71, 81
Webb, Beatrice 98, 102
Webb, Sidney 98, 102
West Germany 87–96, 114, 116
West Hougham 22–3
Westminster, Palace of 31
White Horse Inn (Lehar) 88
White House 20
Why You Should Be A Socialist
    (Strachey) 63
Wight, Martin 123–4, 139
Wigram, Sir Clive (later Lord) 32
Williams, Alan Lee 108
Wilson, Harold 129
Wiltshire 59–60
Windsor 76
Windsor, Duke of 35
    see also Edward, Prince of Wales
        (David, later Edward VIII, then
        Duke of Windsor)
Winged Victory of Samothrace 120
Winterhalter, Franzer Xaver 121
Woodford 63
Woolf, Leonard 103
Woolf, Virginia 103
Woolworth's 13
Worth, House of 121
WRNS (Women's Royal Naval
    Service) 16, 132
Wye, River 52

Yale Centre for British Art 111
York, Duchess of 1
York, Duke of (later George VI) 1,
    2, 30
'You Are My Heart's Delight' 36
The Young Carthaginian (Henty) 41

Z Reservists 134, 135–7
Zugspitze 95